Be Prepared

HOW TO LIGHT A WET MATCH AND 199 OTHER USEFUL THINGS TO KNOW

...CTURES...FIX A PUNCTURE...LEAD A HORSE...TACKL
...WD...GET BY IN FIVE LANGUAGES...CHOOSE A CAMP
...NT PEG...FIX A TENT...MAKE A HUT...SECURE A ROP
...P REGISTER...DRY WET BOOTS...MAKE A SIMPLE FIR
...TURES...SHARPEN A KNIFE...OPEN A STUCK PENKNI
...N...EASE STUCK PAIN...TREAT BLISTERS...REMOVE A S
...VE...SHARPEN A SAW...ADJUST A CISTERN BALL V
...JOIN WIRE NEATLY...REMOVE A TIGHT SCREW...US
...GES...MAKE A REMOVABLE MOUSEHOLE...OIL A LOCK
...EEP...BUILD A PLATE RACK...HANG A PICTURE...FIT
...LF...MEND BROKEN LEATHER...MEND A BROKEN CH
...RANCE...MAKE A SELF-MADE TIE...PRESS YOUR TR
...RS...BRUSH YOUR SLEEVE...BE A SMART DRESS...AV
...TODENT SITUATIONS...MAKE A PAPER CUP...REMOVE C
...M...REMOVE THE RIGHT SAUCEPAN...MAKE LIGHT
...KT...CALCULATE THE HEIGHT OF A TREE...MEASURE T
...DED...ROUTES...REMEMBER KNOTS...WRITE A POS
...CORRECTLY...FLY FOR FREE...PRESS FLOWERS...GET
...HAIR...KNOW YOUR FLAG...MAKE A SLIDING GRIP...S
...E...PLAY SOME CRICKET SHOTS...MAKE A TUMBLE
...TER...JUMP...BE BRAVE...OVERCOME DIZZINESS...D
...E AND FENCE...HOLD AN EEL...MAKE A FIRE BEFOR
...NTURE...LEAD A HORSE...TACKLE THE UNDERGROU
...NGUAGE...CHOOSE A CAMPING GROUND...MAKE A T
...T...MAKE A HUT...SECURE A ROPE...MAKE A CAMP
...GISTER...DRY WET BOOTS...MAKE A SIMPLE FIRELI
...TE...OPEN A STUCK PENKNIFE...USE A LINE...U
...STERS...REMOVE A SPLINTER WITH A NEEDLE...RE
...G VALVE...MAKE NEAT TERMINALS...MAKE A BUSY
...OW...KEEP OUT DRAUGHTS...MAKE A WEATHER
...RY...OIL A LOCK...MAKE A FLOWER POT HOLDER...FIT
...K...HANG A PICTURE...MAKE A PICTURE FRAME...FI
...THER...MEND A BROKEN LEATHER...MAKE A SELF-MA
...DE TIE...PRESS YOUR TROUSERS...BRUSH YOUR
...VE...BE SMART DRESS...AVOID A TIGHT...REMOVE
...CUP...CARRY CUPS...MAKE A LIGHTER GRIP...ADJ
...TER...BALL VALVE...JOIN A WIRE OUT OF A NEEDL
...REE...MEASURE THE WIDTH OF A RIVER...MAKE A PO
...NTS...WRITE A POEM...TELL THE AGE OF BIRDS...TE
...WERS...GET A JOB...VOTE...WALK ON THE RIGHT SID
...KET CODE...SIGNAL BY MORSE CODE...MNEMONIC
...NCHING BAG...GET A STRONG GRIP...DO BREAST STRO

Be Prepared

HOW TO LIGHT A WET MATCH AND 199 OTHER USEFUL THINGS TO KNOW

SCOUTING SINCE 1907

SIMON & SCHUSTER
ILLUSTRATED

London · New York · Sydney · Toronto · New Delhi

A CBS COMPANY

First published in Great Britain by
Simon & Schuster UK Ltd, 2013

A CBS COMPANY

1 3 5 7 9 10 8 6 4 2

SIMON & SCHUSTER
ILLUSTRATED BOOKS
Simon & Schuster UK Ltd
222 Gray's Inn Road
London WC1X 8HB

www.simonandschuster.co.uk
Simon & Schuster Australia, Sydney
Simon & Schuster India, New Delhi

Editor: Sam Carter
The Scout Association: Chris James
Additional Illustrations: Jolyon Braime
Designer: Richard Proctor
Cover Design: Corinna Farrow

A CIP catalogue record for this book is available from the British Library

ISBN 978-1-47110-248-6

Printed and bound in the UK by CPI Group (UK) Ltd, Croydon, CR0 4YY

Disclaimer

Much of this book is reproduced from historical sources and in no way represents current good practice or official advice. Members of Scouting are referred to www.scouts.org.uk/por for up-to-date guidance. The Scout Association and the publisher disclaim any liability for any injury, accidents or loss that may occur as a result of information or instructions given in this book.

Children should be supervised by an adult at all times. Always use your best common sense, wear appropriate safety gear, stay within the law and local rules and be considerate of other people.

Metric and Imperial measurements

Much of the material in this book dates from a time when the Imperial system was in use. Here is a handy conversion chart to modern metric measurements:

Length	Mass	Volume and capacity
1 inch = 2.5 cm	1 kg = 2.2 lb	2 pints = 1 litre
1 foot = 30 cm	1 lb = 0.5 kg	1 gallon = 4.5 litres
1 mile = 1.6 km	1 ounce (oz)	
5 miles = 8 km	= 25 grams	
3 feet = 1 metre		

Imperial system

Length	Mass
1 foot (ft) = 12 inches	1 pound (lb) = 16 ounces (oz)
1 yard = 3 feet	1 stone = 14 pounds

Volume and capacity
1 gallon = 8 pints (pt)

"A human being should be able to change a nappy, conn a ship, design a building, write a sonnet, balance accounts, build a wall, set a bone, comfort the dying, take orders, give orders, cooperate, act alone, solve equations, analyze a new problem, pitch manure, program a computer, cook a tasty meal, fight efficiently, die gallantly."

Robert A. Heinlein, born 1907
(the same year as Scouting)

Foreword

*L*ife is full of challenges. Whether it's trying to mend a puncture by the side of a busy road, light a wet match or stand on a moving train, sometimes things are not always as straightforward as they could be. That's where a book likes this comes in. Drawing on the wit and wisdom of Scouts down the ages, *Be Prepared* contains both remarkable and reliable advice for a smoother journey through life.

Have you ever wondered how to vault a fence, throw a lasso or make your own sandals? Even if you haven't, I bet you will be curious to know how. Want to discover how a cabbage leaf can be used to treat a blister? I thought so. Many of the hints and tips come from old issues of *The Scout,* a periodical for younger members, purchased with hard-won pocket money along with their ginger beer and liquorice allsorts. Of course it seems quaintly written now, but that doesn't make it any less useful.

Ideal for anyone who wants to know how their predecessors faced up to trials and tribulations, this book is a fascinating window into a forgotten era of good humour and common sense. It is also an insight into a more civilised age of courtesy and chivalry. Some of these things shouldn't be outdated at all. Need to improvise a tie in an emergency? You'll find the answer here.

One thing you'll notice throughout this book is the importance of basic values: be kind, be helpful and above all try to be good. That was the case then and it still holds true today. Sometimes the most important thing when trying to solve a problem is believing it can be done. You'll learn the value of improvisation, having an optimistic outlook and being self-reliant. Having a 'can do' attitude is not something new.

Of course Scouting has changed quite a bit down the years.

For one thing, we have over 65,000 girls in Scouting now. But there's plenty of wisdom in this book that stands the test of time. Scouts pride themselves on their sense of adventure, their practical skills and knowledge and it's great to see so much of this in one place. The next time you need to remove a splinter, hang a picture or even greet the monarch, you'll be better prepared.

Bear Grylls
Chief Scout

Be an
Intrepid Traveller

We all know that travel broadens the mind, but it also poses its own problems and pitfalls. Different countries and cultures have different ways of doing things. A friendly greeting in one country can be interpreted as a gesture of great disrespect in another. Be sensitive and prepared to listen, learn and share. More important than seeing the great cathedrals, castles and museums of the world is to get to know its people. As Tim Cahill once said, "A journey is best measured in friends, rather than miles."

How to vault a gate and fence

There is nothing the real athlete dislikes so much as to see someone straddle over a gate. It is ungainly, and jars with all his ideas of graceful motion. It is not everybody who can vault or jump a gate in a clean, graceful fashion, and here the Scout's staff should come in handy. It can be used in much the same fashion as the pole-jumper uses his pole. When you come to the gate or fence, place one hand upon it, and the other at the top of your staff. Then a slight spring should easily carry you over the obstacle. Take care to keep the legs together when vaulting. After a little practice it should be possible to take the gate without slackening speed when approaching it at a run. Please be sure that the staff is strong enough to support your weight; if in doubt, do not use it.

> *It is not everybody who can vault or jump a gate in a clean, graceful fashion*

Vaulting a Fence

When vaulting a fence always make your leap with the foot on the same side as the hand which grasps the fence. If you grasp the top rail with your left hand, your left foot should go over first; so if you grasp with your right hand, your right foot should lead. Otherwise, you may fall heavily astride the bar and injure yourself. Do not put your full weight on the hand but rely mainly on your spring.

How to hold an eel

If during your holidays at the seaside you indulge in the piscatorial arts and catch an eel, you will have some trouble in holding it unless you know the "knack". No difficulty will be experienced if you grasp it in the manner shown, for by doing so the slippery customer is easily kept still, and the hook can be extracted. A sharp tap administered with his tail on any hard substance handy will keep him quiet for quite a considerable time.

How to make a bike holder

When a bicycle is kept against the wall the constant scratching of the handle bar makes an unsightly mark. The illustration shows a method whereby such damage can be avoided. Two pieces of wood, a hinge, and a clutch fitted to the long piece of wood to hold the crossbar of the cycle are all that are required.

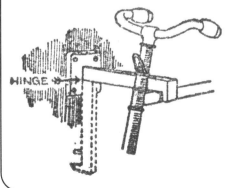

Another advantage of this holder is that it is not in the way when the bicycle is absent, for it can be bent down parallel with the wall.

How to keep mud out of your bike bearings

In wet weather cyclists will find that water and mud runs down the wheel spokes of the machine, and works into the bearings, causing them to wear out much more rapidly than they would if protected.

To prevent this, cut circles of soft felt to act as washers and fit these on to the spindle, as shown. Washers of this type will be too soft to check the action of the wheel, but they will soak up any moisture that would otherwise reach the bearings.

FELT DISCS

The washers should be removed occasionally and the dirt washed out, after which they may be replaced unless too worn.

Puncture tips

If, when cycling a long way from home, you have a puncture and are handicapped by not possessing something that holds water, you will find that the top part of your bell makes an excellent holder.

This dome, when filled with water, is just big enough to hold sufficient water to find a puncture.

How to prevent punctures

Punctures are always a nuisance, especially when the cyclist is on tour. Here is a simple arrangement which will be found very beneficial in preventing these. Before starting on a journey, fasten a piece of twine round the stays of the mudguards about a quarter of an inch from the tyre. When a thorn is picked up it is caught by this barrier of string and thrown out before it has time to do any damage. If preferred, the twine could be attached to the forks instead of the mudguards.

How to fix a puncture

Nothing annoys a cyclist more than a burst, and though we cannot tell an infallible way of avoiding these troublesome occurrences, the hint given here will be found useful when the unavoidable has happened. If a patch is stuck over a slit in an inner tube in the ordinary way (Fig. 1) the hole will possibly lengthen and great annoyance be caused. If, however, a small circular hole is made at each end of the slit, as in Fig. 2 before the patch is applied, further splitting will be prevented.

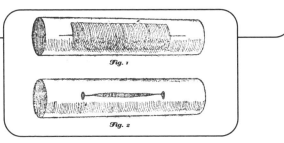

Fig. 1

Fig. 2

Testing the valve

Many cyclists, when their tyre shows signs of deflation, imagine that the cause of the trouble is a puncture. Then they hastily remove the outer cover and put the inner tube through water when, sometimes, to the surprise of the unfortunate cyclist, no leakage can be discovered. When the valve is tested, however, it is found that the fault lies there. Why go to all this trouble? It will be found very useful always to test the valve before commencing operations on the tyre. A very effective method

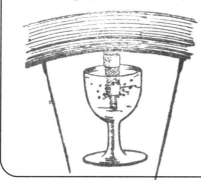

of doing this is to fill an eggcup with water and place it over the valve, as shown in the illustration. Should the air be escaping at that spot bubbles will rise in the water and betray the fact.

Prevent cycling accidents

Before you mount your bicycle be sure that the ends of your boot laces are knotted on the outside, so as to be away from the chain, gear wheels and cranks.

Many an accident has been caused through laces becoming loose and entwining about moving parts of the machine.

Native American markings

Native Americans have many ingenious methods of marking a trail, and here are two of the signs in practice among the tribes. The first three illustrations represent "grass signs". A bunch of grass tied in an upright position signifies "This is the trail," with the end pointing to the left, "Turn to the left," and with the end pointing to the right, "Turn to the right." In the three bottom illustrations are shown

Native Americans have many ingenious methods of marking a trail

signs made by blazing on trees, similar to the grass signs. The small square in the centre of the tree means, "This is the trail," with a large oblong blazing to the left of it, "Turn to the left;" with the large blazing to the right, "Turn to the right."

How to ride a horse

You should learn this little verse so that you can observe the rules when riding:

Your head and your heart keep up;
Your hands and your heels keep down;
Your knees keep close to the horse's sides;
And your elbows close to your own.

How to tie a horse

When you have to leave a horse and cart standing a moment, don't fasten the animal to a gate or post by the reins. If the horse pulls at the reins at all, and draws them tight, his head is pulled back, as the reins pass through the rings of the collar and saddle harness. So the horse naturally begins to "back", and the harder he backs, the tighter the reins pull him in, till something has to give way.

Tying a horse in this manner one does once but never again. However, it is best not to do it that once, as the results are usually disastrous.

The only way to fasten a horse in harness is by a separate rope or chain straight from the bridle to the post.

How to lead a horse

If you happen to be leading a horse, there is always a possibility of getting your feet trodden on if you don't know the right way to lead him.

When Dobbin puts his left foot forward and you are leading him by your right hand, you should put your right foot forward, as the fellow in the illustration is doing. The animal doesn't get a chance to tread on your left foot then.

This idea is reversed, of course, when leading the horse with your left hand.

This little picture clearly shows how you should lead a horse.

How to tackle the underground

When you are in a crowded train or tram, you may lose your balance unless you are holding on to a strap. Here is a way to prevent this. As the train commences to move you should stand, with legs apart, facing the window, as shown by the Scout in Figure A.

How to stand on a moving train

As the train gathers in motion, reverse, and stand facing the driver, with feet firmly apart, for the train has a tendency to sway from side to side. Figure B will explain this. There is no need for you to stand when there are seats vacant, as the Scout in our illustration is doing, for the artist has purposely left the carriage empty so as to make this quite clear to you.

When the train begins to slow down you turn again to position one. If you follow this hint you will feel none the worse for your stand in the train.

Figure A   *Figure B*

How to stand in a crowd

When standing in a crowd, there is always a danger of people being badly crushed by the mass of people around you, and so having a rib broken.

To prevent this, you should keep your arms in the position shown in our illustration and not at your sides as most people would in the circumstances.

By keeping your arms raised in the manner shown, you have them free and can quickly push through the crowd should you wish to.

How to get by in five languages

French

Do you have any rooms available?
Avez-vous des chambres libres?

Is breakfast included?
Le petit-déjeuner est-il inclus?

"JE SUIS PERDU"

What time is breakfast?
À quelle heure est le petit-déjeuner?

Where is the loo?
Où sont les toilettes?

Where is the bus stop?
Où est l'arrêt de bus?

I'm lost.
Je suis perdu.

Do you speak English?
Parlez-vous anglais?

Italian

Do you have any rooms available?
Avete camere libere?

Is breakfast included?
La colazione è inclusa?

What time is breakfast?
A che ora è la colazione?

Where is the loo?
Dov'è la toilette?

Where is the bus stop?
Dove si trova la fermata del bus?

I'm lost.
Mi sono persa.

Do you speak English?
Parli inglese?

German

Do you have any rooms available?
Sind noch Zimmer frei?

Is breakfast included?
Ist das Frühstück mit inbegriffen?

What time is breakfast?
Wann gibt es Frühstück?

Where is the loo?
Wo ist die Toilette?

Where is the bus stop?
Wo ist die Bushaltestelle?

I'm lost.
Ich habe mich verirrt.

Do you speak English?
Sprechen Sie Englisch?

Spanish

Do you have any rooms available?
¿Hay habitaciones libres?

Is breakfast included?
¿Está incluido el desayuno?

What time is breakfast?
¿A qué hora es el desayuno?

Where is the loo?
¿Dónde está el baño?

Where is the bus stop?
¿Dónde está la parada de autobús?

I'm lost.
Estoy perdido.

Do you speak English?
¿Habla usted inglés?

Japanese

Do you have any rooms available?
空いてる部屋ありますか?
Aiteru heya arimasuka?

Is breakfast included?
朝食は付きますか?
Chôshoku wa tsukimasuka?

What time is breakfast?
朝食は何時ですか?
Chôshoku wa nanji desuka?

Where is the loo?
お手洗い(トイレ)はどこですか?
Oh-teh-ah-rah-ee wah DOH-koh dess kah?

I'm lost.
迷子になりました。
Maigo ni nari-mashita.

Do you speak English?
英語が話せますか?
EHH-goh gah hah-nah-seh-mahs-KAH?

Be
Adventurous

Baden-Powell himself said that "life without adventure would be deadly dull". No matter how young or old you are, with the right attitude, every day is an adventure. Walk a different way to work or school. Speak to someone new, try a new hobby. Go camping! The natural world is an amazing – and free – adventure playground; instead of watching television this Saturday afternoon, get the bikes out of the shed, pack a sandwich and head off into the unknown (or at least into the next village). You don't need to jump out of helicopters to have an adventure, but a little risk-taking every once in a while is good for the mind, body and soul.

How to choose a camping ground

Look over it on a cold, wet, wintry day, then you will see it at its worst. If you can then see any attractions, you may rest assured it will be an attractive spot in the summer-time.

Also do not choose a spot that is down in a hollow; choose a spot that has some shelter from the prevailing wind; and not by any means the least things to consider are the nearness of water and fuel and the view. There is nothing more lowering to the spirits in camp than a depressing view.

It is always wise to find out the history of the water supply. There have been cases where the camp water supply has come from a stream that has taken in refuse from a sewerage farm or chemical works.

Very rarely does one get a good camping ground with water laid on, and it is a wise plan to get water as near to the chosen spot as possible, otherwise some of your fellows will spend all their time carrying water.

Always be very certain of having permission before taking any wood for fires, and never cut growing timber or break down hedges, fences or gates. Also, if your quarters are on farm land, never have a fire in the stack yard.

Don'ts for Campers

- Don't forget to slacken your guy ropes before turning in, as the dew tightens them.
- Don't chop trees down without permission. In any case get dead wood; live, green stuff won't burn.
- Don't go near canals or rivers if you have been told to keep away.
- Don't grumble if your leader asks you to fetch milk from the farm while the others are playing cricket.
- Don't forget to have a jolly good time, wear a smile, and lend a hand!

How to make a tent for your garden

On warm nights many of you would, no doubt, like to sleep out in your gardens, but do not like to do so without some kind of covering.

The illustration shows how a serviceable "bivouac" can be rigged up on your lawn. First get two forked sticks either from your own garden or from the nearest woods, and drive them into the ground about seven feet apart.

Put a long pole across these, and you have the framework of your "bivvy" complete.

Hang a large camp blanket over this pole, and instead of keeping it in position with the aid of guy ropes and pegs, roll a log on to each end of the blanket as shown in the picture.

These logs will keep the blanket taut, and although the structure will not stand any really bad weather, it will make an admirable shelter and serve your purpose quite well when the weather is warm.

How to erect a bell tent

Lay the tent on the ground, door uppermost, put the pole together, and fit it well into the crown of the tent, after which raise it. One person must hold the pole upright, while another goes round pegging. The four red runners on the ropes should be pegged down first, so as to square the tent. Be most careful to see that the door is not facing the prevailing winds, or the occupants will have a lively time of it. After erection to one's liking, dig round the bottom of the curtain a small trench or gully, to take away the rain from the tent. At intervals round the bottom of the curtain there are small rope loops; these are also for pegs, to be used at night, or during wet weather. If it is fine the curtain may be rolled up. Don't forget to slacken the ropes if it is wet, before turning in at night, as if this is not done, the tent becoming taut will either pull the pegs out of the ground, or the pole will find its way through the crown.

How to drive a tent peg

How many know the right way to drive a tent peg? It looks a simple matter to do, yet it is wonderful how many do it wrongly, and what dim results occur when wind and rainstorms come upon a camp where tent pegs have been badly driven into the ground. The accompanying diagram shows how it should not be driven and how it should be driven.

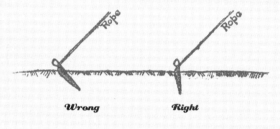

Wrong   *Right*

How to fix a tent in loose ground

All Scouts who have experienced the difficulty of tent pegging in loose gravel will welcome the following device. To prevent your tent peg shifting in the sand or gravel, make a hole about two feet deep and drive your first peg into it, as shown in the illustration, fixing the rope firmly to the peg. Then in the usual way, drive in the second peg, wind the rope round it, and the operation is complete, and the tent unquestionably secure. A piece of wood about four or more inches long will take a hold quite as effective as the usual peg, provided it is sunk in the manner described.

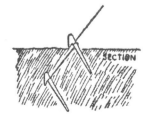

How to make a hut

The Australian Bow-gunuogh makes an excellent substitute for a tent and is very simple in construction. It resembles the tent made with the aid of Scout staves and canvas squares, but of course it can be constructed on a much larger scale.

Cut two poles to a height of, say, six feet with a strong fork at one end and pointed at the other. Drive them firmly into the ground six feet apart. Cut a pole eight feet long and let it rest in the forks of the two upright poles as in Fig. 1.

Then, cutting a number of eight-foot poles, bind them to the ridge pole on each side so that they cross in the manner shown in Fig. 2, and at an angle of sixty degrees with the forked pole. The whole is then covered with a thick thatch of bracken and branches. When finished it should make a serviceable shelter.

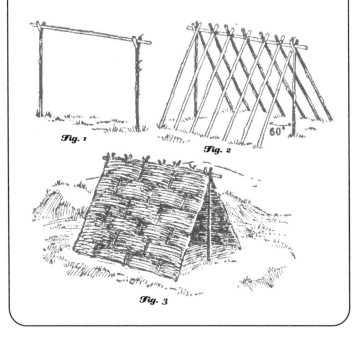

Fig. 1

Fig. 2

Fig. 3

How to secure a rope

To secure a rope's end to the ground so that it will stand considerable strain, it is necessary to drive in at least three stakes and connect them in such a way that all bear an equal part of

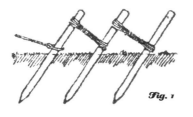

the strain. Fig. I shows the method. First drive in your stakes securely in the line in which the strain will be borne; then lash the first stake to the second (as

Fig. 1

shown in the illustration), the second to the third, and so on. The rope can then be tied to the first stake, and the strain it bears will be distributed between the others. For additional security or a greater strain, it is advisable to drive in three stakes together in the first instance, two in the second, and one in the third (Fig. 2). Fig. 3 shows what is termed an "earth anchorage" – that is,

Fig. 2

a log buried in the ground to resist the strain of ropes or cables that may be made fast to it. Upon the depth to which it is buried

depends the strain it is able to resist.

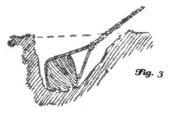

Fig. 3

How to make a camp oven

To cook food in camp properly, you must have the right utensils and the best possible fireplace. There are some really splendid ideas in this article.

By Major J. T. Gorman

Many people think that it is impossible to get beyond a stew in camp cooking.

This is quite a mistake; and you need no more than just the camp kettle, or, for single individuals, the mess-tin, to enable you to boil, fry, and even bake, as well as stew your meat.

So the first kind of camp oven which I will describe is the camp kettle, or mess-tin, used in this manner.

The Camp Kettle

In the first place, put some fat or dripping at the bottom of the vessel, and upon this place some clean, smooth stones. Lay your piece of meat for baking upon these stones, whether it be a large joint in a camp kettle or a small steak or chop in a mess-tin.

Set the camp kettle on the hottest part of the fire at first, and let it stand there for about a quarter of an hour, after which move it to a cooler place at the side, and let the meat go on cooking slowly. There is no need to continually drop the fat over the meat. The action of the fat upon the stones in the vessel acts as a self-basting arrangement.

Roughly, from eighteen to twenty minutes to a pound of meat is the time required for baking – like this – in a camp kettle.

The Camp Oven

Another way of using the camp kettle, or dixie, as an oven is as follows:

"Camp" Oven

Dig a hole in a bank, or in a prepared mound of earth, large enough to hold the dixie, lying on its side, with the open end outwards, as shown here.

Place inside the vessel sufficient fuel to burn for about an hour, and light this wood. When it is reduced to ashes take all these embers out, except a small quantity, put in your baking-dish, with the meat; cover the opening of the camp kettle with its lid, and plug up all the crevices with earth.

If the oven is required for pastry, let it cool down for about two minutes before putting it in; but meat should be placed in the camp kettle directly the embers are withdrawn. A little longer time is required to cook meat in this way than in an ordinary oven; roughly, about half an hour to a pound of meat or a little less.

Both these methods can be carried out, on a smaller scale, with mess-tins, or billies. A seven-pound biscuit tin can be substituted for the camp kettle, burying it in earth as before.

The Hole-in-the-Ground Oven

The most useful of all camp ovens, however, is the "hole-in-the-ground" oven. It is not at all difficult to make, and will cook anything which can be accomplished in an ordinary kitchen oven, taking about the same time to do it.

Here is how to set about making a "hole-in-the-ground".

Select a place where the ground is as dry as possible, and dig a trench, with the sides sloping inwards, about eight or nine inches in depth. This hole must be large enough to take your baking-dish, which should be about twelve inches in length, by eight in width, and three in depth. Such a dish is invaluable in camp, both for baking meat and for making cakes and pies.

Now make an inch-high ridge all round above the ground-level.

You will need a sheet of iron or tin, a bit bigger than the oven-hole, to lay on the top of it, as a cover. This can be obtained very easily.

"Hole-in-the-ground" Oven

When the oven is dug, light a wood fire inside it, and let it burn until it is just a pile of red embers. Take these embers out, putting them on the iron sheet; place the baking-dish, with the meat, pudding or cake in it, inside the hole, cover it down with the sheet of iron, and plug round the crevices with mud, earth or moss.

Then keep the fire burning on the top of the sheet of metal, replenishing it with wood as often as necessary and never allowing it to die down.

In the case of a very large piece of meat, it is best to remove the top of the oven at half-time, turn the joint, and replace the cover and the fire as before.

This hole-in-the-ground oven can also be built above the ground, with stones, turves or bricks, and will be found just as effective.

A Sawdust Stove

If you can obtain a cylindrical tin, about twenty-four inches high, and from eight to ten inches in diameter, you can easily make a sawdust stove, which is a wonderful asset in a camp. The four-gallon tins used for the export of petrol are exactly suitable for this purpose, if you can get one.

Four holes, each about two inches in diameter, are first bored in the circumference of the tin, at equal distances round the bottom and about three inches up.

Through these holes two sticks are inserted, fitting rather loosely, and going right through from one side to the other, with the ends protruding at each side.

Then insert a third stick from the top of the tin, in such a way that the end of it rests on the point of junction of the other two, in the middle of the tin.

Whilst this stick is held in this position, pack the tin very tightly with sawdust, filling it as full as it will hold. Then withdraw the sticks, and, if the sawdust has been packed in tightly enough, the holes left by the sticks will remain quite clear.

Put a piece of lighted paper into one of the holes near the base of the tin, and your sawdust cooker is now in full blast, and will burn for from eight to twelve hours without any kind of attention.

The camp kettle or vessel, containing whatever you want to cook, stands upon the top of the tin, and if you wish you can leave a stock-pot simmering for a whole day.

At the end of twelve hours or so the sawdust will be consumed, but before using the oven again, it must be re-made.

How to make a camp grill

In the illustration is shown a camp grill which can be very easily constructed. The only material required is a piece of fairly stout steel wire; about three yards should suffice, as the grill will not need to be large. With the aid of a pair of pliers cut off three or four straight pieces of wire (A), then construct the two sides, making a ring at intervals for the bars to pass through; and for each outside bar make the extended supports (B) to prevent the sides collapsing. The advantage of this grill is that when not in use the bars can be withdrawn, and the whole affair may be packed flat into a small space.

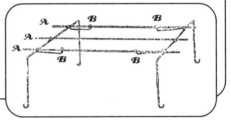

To keep food warm

Scouting is a thing calculated to give one a good appetite, and it is rather annoying when returning to camp, after a good morning's work, to find that the too zealous cook has allowed the dinner to get cold. Many Scouts prefer to eat straight from their "billies" but whether food is eaten from plates or cans, it is sure to get cold if left to stand too long. To remedy this evil, you may get a box large enough to hold vessels containing the Patrol's food supply. If this box is filled with straw, and the plates or "billies" are placed in it until needed, they will keep warm for a very considerable time.

How to make a hammock

If your father keeps a fruit shop, you can get an apple barrel very easily. If he has nothing to do with this trade, try to get a barrel from the shop where your mother buys her fruit. If you are unsuccessful there, try to get any sort of barrel, as long as it is not too cumbersome.

When you have obtained the barrel, take off the hoops; then remove the nails – but don't throw them away. You never know when those nails may be useful.

Eventually you will find that all that remains of the barrel are the staves. Take each one and make a mark about three inches from the top, and also three inches from the bottom.

When you have done this, bore two holes at top and bottom at the mark you have made, as shown in the picture.

You do the same thing with each stave. Now can you see how they will form a hammock? No? Well, read on a little further then.

Now get a length of rope, about eighteen to twenty feet will be sufficient, and thread it through the holes along one side, then leave a couple of feet in the form of a loop, and begin threading back along the bottom edge.

When you reach the two ends again, tie with a – well, what knot? Reef! Yes, that's right.

Now your hammock is ready. When you wish to use it, find two suitable trees, and get two lengths of rope. Pass one piece through the loop at one end of the hammock, and tie to the tree with a – well, what knot? Another reef! Good! You do the same thing at the other end.

All you have to do now is to get a few cushions, take out with you a copy of *Scouting*, jump into the hammock – and enjoy yourself.

Simple, isn't it?

One way of dining in camp

Provided the soil is dry and not loose or uneven, a very good mess table for use in camp can be made as follows: dig a fair sized oval trench, about two feet deep, leaving an oblong space in the centre, which forms the table, and then sit round on the ground, with your legs in the trench, and your plate of food in front of you, as shown in the illustration.

How to make a camp bedstead

The bed which is about to be described should prove a useful article for cyclist Scouts owing to the ease with which it can be carried from place to place. It can be constructed quite easily. The first requirement is a piece of waterproof canvas from six to seven feet long and about two-and-a-half feet broad, on one side of which should be buttoned a blanket of the same size. Then a piece of waterproof canvas about five and a half feet long, with a blanket buttoned on to one side of it, should be sewn to the other piece of canvas, blanket sides together. In the illustration the smaller canvas is shown sewn on three sides, in the manner of a sack, but, in order that the blankets may be unbuttoned and aired, it is advisable to secure the two longest sides by means of hooks, buttons or cords. It will be noticed in the illustration that, after fixing the top canvas on, the underneath and larger piece protrudes by about one and a half feet (A B). This is for the head to rest on. It is now necessary to construct a hood for the head. This can be made from a piece of glazed linen, about four feet long by one and a half wide, buttoned to each side of the projecting under canvas and supported by two pieces of bamboo – one piece stuck in the ground, and the other tied to it horizontally (C) and keeping up the head covering. The small triangle shows the front view of the hood, D is the space for the head, and F the bamboo rod. The base, of course, is two and a half feet wide, and, as the length of the canvas is four feet, each side will measure two feet. By making pockets underneath the bed, legs could be inserted and the bed raised from the ground, as shown in the picture, if desired. A comfortable pillow can be made from dried grass.

How to make an outdoor bedstead

Why not make the little bed shown in the sketch? It is very comfortable and can be put together quite easily.

The materials required are four stakes about three feet long, sharpened at one end; two pieces of strong-board, three feet long by three inches wide; a few nails; and some cord.

Sink the stakes in the ground, then nail the pieces of wood to them as shown. Take a stretcher, place it across the supports, and lash it firmly on the four corners. The bed is now ready for use.

To boil the pot quickly

A good Scout competition consists not only in seeing who can light a fire with one match, but in finding out also who can boil a pailful of water quickest. In a competition held by a camping club, the members were each supplied with a tin pail, one match and an axe. They were lined up, and, at a given signal, they had to run and cut their logs, fill their pails, light their fires, and start the water boiling. The winning member accomplished this in the manner illustrated. He took a pole, pointed it, and made a notch near the top. He then drove the stake slantwise into the ground in such a manner that when the pail handle was placed in the notch the flames of the fire would have full play on the bottom of the pail.

Camp drinking water

There is a common belief that clear water is pure water. Scouts who are going to camp should be very careful about their drinking supply.

While water that looks dirty is sometimes harmless – peat colours water, but does not harm it to any great extent – danger may exist although the water is sparkling and clear.

Scouts should bear in mind that a very simple and effective safeguard is to boil the liquid for five or ten minutes before using it for drinking purposes.

A novel sundial

A novel sundial, which will form a very interesting experiment for you whilst in camp, can be made if a bell tent be erected with the aperture due south. When this is done, you will get a bar of sunshine which will travel round the interior of your tent during the day, and, by marking off with your watch the various spots which this bar of light strikes upon at different hours of the morning and afternoon, you will obtain a reliable sundial for use on other bright days.

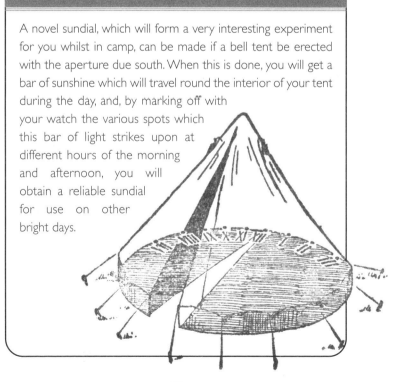

Be
Able to Survive

The chances of you being born at all were incredibly slim, so don't waste your one opportunity by making a silly mistake. If you find yourself in a predicament then you need to be prepared. Being able to light a fire in the rain or stop a bicycle in an emergency could be the difference between life and death. Often things are not as bad as they first seem. As Daniel Defoe remarked in *Robinson Crusoe*, "The fear of danger is ten thousand times more terrifying than danger itself."

How to tell the viper

The only reptiles of the serpent tribe known in Great Britain are the grass snake, the blind-worm, and the viper or adder; of these three the viper alone is venomous. As the adder is uncommon, it may be well to describe it.

1 The full-grown viper is much smaller than the common snake.

2 The marks on the back of the viper are zigzagged, or lozenged, and joined with one another, while in the common snake they are distinct from each other, and are spots and dashes.

3 Note the angle of the jaws of the viper as compared to the snake.

4 The eye of the snake is large and round, while that of the viper is smaller, and the pupil is like that of a cat's eye. The eyebrow overhangs the eye.

5 The viper has a receding chin.

6 The viper remains coiled up ready to spring.

Common grass snake

The viper

How to dry wet boots

Wet boots should never be put near the fire, but should be filled with dry oats which will absorb all the damp from the leather. As the oats absorb the moisture, they swell and fill the boots. They therefore fulfil the duties of drying the boots and keeping them in good shape at the same time.

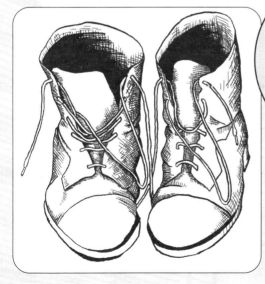

Wet boots should never be put near the fire, but should be filled with dry oats

Wood for the campfire

Any kind of wood will burn, but any kind of wood will not do for the campfire. Woodmen know this well. When making their midday fires, they are very careful to avoid certain trees. They never take branches of larch, willow, poplar, horse-chestnut or lime. They will tell you that such woods are useless because they merely smoulder and do not burn brightly.

The skilled forester kindles his fire with dry grasses or dead twigs of spruce. The branches at the base of a spruce tree are so well sheltered by the dense cover overhead, that they can almost always be obtained dry enough to burn. But after a spell of wet weather it sometimes happens that even the spruce is too damp to kindle; the forester then hunts around until he finds a resinous piece of pine wood or bark which takes fire with a little coaxing.

To keep a fire going, beech is the best fuel, though birch is almost as good. Oak also burns splendidly, but the good woodman rarely makes use of it. He regards it as too valuable.

There are two other things he never does. He never puts rotten wood on his fire, and he never uses paper!

How to light a wet match

If your only wax match falls into a puddle just as you are preparing to light your campfire you need not despair of striking it – even though it may have been in the water for quite a minute. Take and dry it roughly on your handkerchief or coat and then stick it in your hair. Leave it there for a minute and it will come out perfectly dry again.

MATCH

Fire lighting tips

Hard wood makes the hottest coals and burns longest, whilst wood containing pitch lights quickly, burns readily and gives a hot blaze.

Splinters from the inside of logs will burn better than the outside, and are, therefore, more useful for starting a fire.

Build your fire where the wind will cause a good draught.

If your fireplace is in an open spot where the wind is variable, dig the fire trenches like the spokes of a wheel and block with stones those not in use, changing the trenches to suit the wind.

If a fire is even slightly sheltered from the rain by an overhanging boulder, bank or fallen tree, it will burn throughout a storm.

How to make a simple firelighter

To address Scouts on the subject of fire-lighting seems like carrying coals to Newcastle. Nevertheless, a hint on how to light a grate fire quickly may not come amiss. The illustration shows a thick piece of wood which is cut into shavings at one end. Directly a light is applied to the shavings they catch and set light to the main piece of wood, which otherwise would be difficult to ignite with only the layer of paper at the bottom of the grate. Two or three of these firelighters will start a good fire much quicker than if the wood were laid on in the ordinary way and left to burn through.

How to light a fire without matches

There are often spare minutes where you would like to be doing little odd stunts, picking up various tricks and dodges which are all part of the great game of Scouting and certainly take a place in the training of someone who is trying to follow the trail of the backwoodsmen and pioneers.

Such things as lighting a fire in the Native American way, inventing camp gadgets, making a pair of moccasins, axe cases, a woodcraft knife sheath, hiking gear, belts, hatbands, shirts and Eskimo jumpers are all things that can be done by anyone who has a bit of gumption, and can handle a few simple tools.

If you try your hand at these things whenever you have a few odd moments in camp or elsewhere, there is no reason why you should not keep a permanent record of your skill which might count for points in your Patrol competitions. A good scheme would be to record permanently every sparetime activity on your staff by means of branding.

Nothing is described here which has not actually been made and tried by a Troop of Scouts, so don't say "It can't be done." After all, what one fool has done another jolly well can do – so get busy.

Take fire by friction as an example. It's easy enough if you first of all get the right kind of materials and then know how to use them.

Now if you are half the Scout we take you for you won't buy your fire-making outfit from some Scout "shop" but get down to it and make it yourself, and the first question is "What kind of wood shall I use?" Well, there is no need to import tamarac or balsam fir or any other foreign wood, for it can be done just as well with our native woods such as elm, sycamore or willow. In point of fact the writer has made fire with an old broom-stick and a bit of a Tate sugar-box, so it doesn't really much matter.

All you have to remember is that the wood you use must not be too hard or too full of resin to prevent it crumbling a little when friction is applied, and by far the best wood of this kind is elm. If you are lucky enough to find a dead elm tree fallen over and can get permission to cut off a few pieces from the stump you have got the best possible wood, but if not a few pence will purchase plenty of odd pieces of elm from a friendly undertaker or carpenter and these will do just as well.

Having got your elm, make a flat platform about 6 in. × 2 in. by ½ in. thick.

Then from the same wood make a shaft or spindle about a foot long, shaped rather like a cigar, PLATFORM → with one rather rounded blunt end and one pointed end. It is important that one end should be fairly broad, say ¾ in., in order to get plenty of friction.

Now you want a palm or socket. The best thing for this is a flat stone with a little recessed hole in it, but unless you live at the seaside this may be difficult to find. However, make a note

PALMS

of that for your next seaside camp, and meanwhile you will have to carry on with a wooden palm. You can make this of a thickish piece of wood with a hole bored in it about ½ in. deep. A small knot of wood does pretty well – just a little knob cut off level, with a hole bored in it by the top of a knife. Remember, by the way, to put a little grease in the hole or it will get very hot.

Our next need is a bow. For this any stiff piece of wood will do, but it must be stiff. You want a rigid bow and not a springy one, and you should make it, roughly, two feet long.

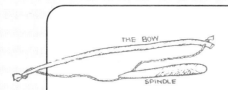

For a thong some strong leather is needed, such as the belting used on small lathes and sewing machines, or you can make a twisted one out of a flat piece of leather, as shown in the sketch, but don't try using your boot-laces – they will only break long before you get a fire.

Note how the thong is attached to the bow by means of three holes bored in it; this enables you to easily adjust the tension on the

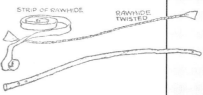

thong, upon which a good deal of your success depends.

All you need now is some tinder. If you are in the wilds you use dry fine grass or moss or bracken or fine shavings, but in more civilised surroundings you can get tow or frazzle out of an old piece of rope to use as tinder.

When you have made your fire-lighting outfit you will want to know how to use it.

Have you ever read *Alone in the Wilderness* by Joseph Knowles? If not, you must. He tells you how to make a fire drill without a knife or axe or anything, and many other things besides, just to prove that we can do what our primitive ancestors had done.

If a Scout was lost in the woods they wouldn't get excited and lose their head as though a towny; they would set to work at once and get the material to produce a fire, even though all the matches may have been used up.

Having made the fire drill outfit the business of getting a fire with it divides up into two parts. First getting a spark and then converting the spark into flame.

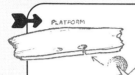

To get the spark take your knife and gouge out a shallow round depression near the edge of the platform. Then cut a V-shaped notch in the edge of the platform reaching nearly to the middle of the shallow hole. See that this V-shaped notch is not too narrow. It should be almost as wide as the board is thick.

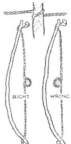

Now fix the thong on to your bow. Just a thumb or figure-eight knot one end and slip through the two holes the other. Don't have it too tight.

Place the platform on a firm smooth surface and hold it down by putting your left heel firmly upon it. Slip the thong round the spindle, taking care that the spindle is outside the thong, and not inside. A glance at the diagrams will make this clear. Then put the base of the spindle on to the hollow in the platform and the point in the palmstone held firmly in the left hand, with the left wrist pressed hard against the skin.

See that the spindle is perfectly upright and then start drilling away with the bow, slowly at first and not putting on too much pressure with the left hand.

In a few moments wood will begin to get hot – so will you – and then smoke begins to curl up. Gradually press harder with the left hand and increase the speed of the bow. You will then have dense clouds of smoke and a little pile of glowing wood dust in the V-shaped notch. Do not disturb this, lay aside the bow, wipe your forehead and try not to be too much overcome by excitement.

There is no need to hurry for the moment. Remember the

motto, "Softly, softly catchee monkey." The little pile of embers will smoulder for some minutes.

Take your tinder of tow or grass or whatever it may be, and make it into a kind of bird's nest about as big as you can conveniently hold in one hand. Then take your pile of glowing wood dust and put it into the bird's nest with the tip of your knife, and close it all up. Blow gently at a safe distance until it catches. If you don't know the glow of satisfaction which comes from your first fire lit without matches you have not yet really lived.

Having done this, you are entitled to brand on your staff the conventional sign of a fire, which you will find at the top of this article.

How to stalk

Here you are shown what to do and what not to do when you are stalking. If you practise these crawls you will soon become proficient in the art of stalking.

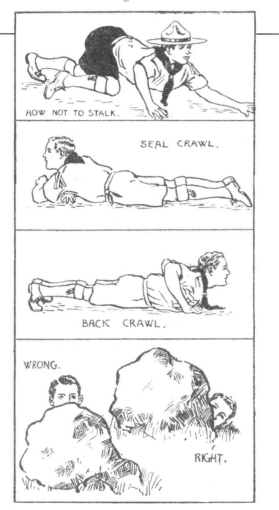

HOW NOT TO STALK.

SEAL CRAWL.

BACK CRAWL.

WRONG.

RIGHT.

How to sharpen a knife

Do not condemn your knife immediately because you cannot put an edge on it. There is a right way and a wrong way of sharpening a knife. Perhaps you have hitherto done it the wrong way. The correct way to sharpen a knife is as follows: pour a few drops of sweet oil on the stone, then, holding the knife so

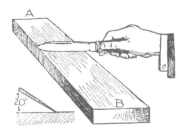

that the blade is at an angle of about twenty to twenty-five degrees to the stone, draw it edge first from A to B, as shown in illustration. On reaching B, turn the knife over and draw it to A, still edge first, to sharpen the other side of the blade. If the blade is laid flat on the stone, the edge is spoilt. If a sufficient angle to the stone is not kept, the edge will be too thin and will very soon become blunt.

In sharpening a razor, it is drawn along the stone back first, but this is not correct for a knife.

How to open a stuck penknife

A stiff penknife blade is often a severe trial to the temper. Try as you will, the usual method of opening it can only be effected

with disastrous results to the finger or thumb nails. The following ingenious method will save both time and nails: fold a small piece of ordinary paper and slip it under the blade in the manner shown in the sketch. On pulling the paper the blade will open quite easily and the sharpest edged knife will not cut through it.

The flower pot sharpener

How do you generally keep your penknife sharp? If you haven't a proper stone, you probably depend upon the kind offices of a chum – or the window-sill! Or, maybe, you don't bother at all.

One of the simplest knife-sharpeners is a flower pot. Just an ordinary clean, red flower pot – the bigger the better.

Lay it on its side, and draw the blade along it with a sweeping motion, first one way and then the other. Test the edge from time to time to see how it is improving. It gets sharp very quickly.

You will find that the flower pot produces a slight roughness on the edge of the blade. So when it is sufficiently keen, remove this by rubbing the blade on a piece of smooth wood, or the family knife-board.

How do you keep your penknife sharp? If you haven't a proper stone, you probably depend on the kind offices of a chum

When crossing a stream

The old hand never crosses a stream bare-footed. He takes off his boots and socks and then puts his boots on again, and, turning up his trousers, wades across. He then takes off his boots and whirls them in the air to get rid off the water in them. The boots are none the worse for their wetting, and are infinitely better than cut feet.

Walking on mud

When a fisherman sets out in pursuit of the elusive eel, he first of all takes the precaution of fastening on what are known as mud pattens to the soles of his long boots. Without these he would sink up to the knees in the soft mud in which eels make their home.

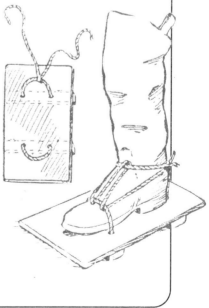

Mud pattens consist of pieces of board about 18 inches long by 12 inches wide, with two cross pieces to strengthen them and keep them from sliding. They are fastened on the feet in the manner shown in the illustration, and by their aid the fisherman can safely negotiate the most treacherous mud patches.

How to use a life-buoy

To anyone who is not acquainted with the method this must seem a useless piece of information. It is not so, however, but is valuable instruction which everyone should know, for no one can tell if there may not come a time when they will require the aid of the life-buoy.

In the hands of the uninitiated the apparatus may prove the reverse of life-saving. He who grabs at the life-buoy in a haphazard manner or tries to enter head first may get into difficulties, and lose his presence of mind completely. It is hard for a drowning man to be methodical, but a method must be employed to obtain the full benefit of the life-buoy. In the first illustration is shown one manner in which the buoy can be entered, for entered it must be.

Place both hands together, on the side of the buoy nearest you, and suddenly bring all your weight to bear on that part. The buoy will immediately jump over you in the manner shown in the second illustration, when all that remains is to put the arms and shoulders through.

Another correct method for those who do not mind a ducking is to grasp one side of the buoy with each hand and suddenly duck the head so as to come up through the centre. The first method is by far the neater as well as being the more comfortable.

What's wrong?

In the picture you will see that the boy climbing the ladder is helping himself up by holding the sides. This is quite wrong, for if his foot slipped he would most certainly slide down with a rush, and might do himself an injury. The rungs form the best grip, and if you hold on to them instead of the sides of the ladder, you have little fear of falling.

What's wrong?

Now what are you going to do? Taking the kettle off, eh? Well, you are a chump! Why, the spout is towards you! You'll be scalded. You should always see that the spout is pointing another way, as kettles – when the water has boiled – have a nasty habit of spitting – yes, and spitting boiling water, too! But if you place the kettle so that the spout is turned the other way, the kettle has to be contented with throwing the water somewhere else – not at you!

What's wrong?

To cut a stick with the knife towards you – as the fellow in the picture is doing – is not only wrong but dangerous, and many nasty accidents have been caused through whittling in this way.

Next time you have to cut a piece of wood or even sharpen a pencil, don't do it as this fellow is doing, but cut it away from you.

Be careful!

It is always advisable to know the temper of any horse before attempting to pat or stroke it. Often the most harmless-looking animal will resent the intended caress with a violent kick or bite. It has, therefore, become necessary to warn people against dangerous animals; and in large horse repositories the stalls of certain horses have pieces of straw rope attached to the posts. This is not in ornamentation, but is intended as a sign that the occupant is not of an amiable disposition. Why the warning should not take the form of a notice that all might understand is incomprehensible, for it is not everybody who would at once recognise a piece of straw rope as a danger signal.

Why red means danger

Red is always used as a danger signal. This is because it is not only the strongest of colours, but it carries a long way. Red is also a constant colour.

For instance, the two colours, blue and green, often run into different shades. Red fixes its unchanging colour upon our vision and our eyes see it as that colour and nothing else.

We have blue skies and seas, green trees and fields, but very little red, so it is therefore a most conspicuous shade and as it is the same colour as fire – and thus to our senses denotes danger, which has the effect of causing alarm – it is most suitable for danger signals.

Be Safe

You should never put yourself in danger.
We have emergency services, so use them. But
occasionally there may be a situation where you
will need to step in and make the difference.
From knowing how to treat a blister or remove
a splinter it's essential you know the basics of
first aid. Of course, you won't learn everything
you need to know in this book, but you will
find some unusual hints and tips and old-
fashioned remedies. Just remember the
old proverb, "Better a thousand times
careful than once dead."

How to check your pulse

Very simply, your pulse is the number of times your heart beats in a single minute. When you are at rest, your pulse will be lower. As you exercise, your pulse will rise as your body demands more oxygen-rich blood.

Before getting down to the checking itself, it's important to take a moment and consider why you are doing it in the first place. The main reasons are to find out: your target heart rate; this will help when exercising as you should always exercise within 60–80 per cent of your target heart rate. This is the most beneficial for health.

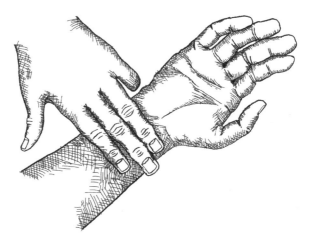

Taking your pulse will also help you discover whether you have an irregular pulse. An irregular pulse is a sign of possible Atrial Fibrillation, for which you should seek medical attention.

Extend your hand, palm upwards. Place just the tips of your index finger, second and third finger on your wrist (as if you are making the Scout salute!) in the small hollow at the base of your thumb. You should feel a firm pulse.

Alternatively, you can put the tips of your index and second fingers on your neck, lightly against your windpipe (either side is fine).

To do something useful with your new skill, count the number of beats in a ten-second time period (using the second hand of a watch or digital stop watch). Now multiply this by six. This will provide your pulse. The normal heart rate for a child is 70–100 beats a minute; for an adult aged 18 or over, it is 60–100 beats a minute.

Use the table below when exercising: if your heart rate falls below the target, speed up. If it rises above the target, slow down.

Age	Target Heart Rate (60-80%)
20	120–170
25	117–166
30	114–162
35	111–157
40	108–153
45	105–149
50	102–145
55	99–140
60	96–136
65	93–132
70	90–128

How to act with a drowning man

There's no harm in knowing just how to tackle a drowning man, although one may never be called upon to act on the knowledge. Our little sketch gives some idea of the correct position of rescuer and rescued. The great thing is to be out of the drowning man's way in case he struggles, and another important thing is to have as much freedom for one's own limbs as possible. So long as the head is sustained above water there is no need to attempt to support more of the body; then swim backwards by vigorous leg strokes till safety is reached.

How to ease burn pain

Sometimes one has the misfortune to place one's finger upon a hot cooking vessel or to get it slightly burned in miscalculating the life of a match. The pain caused is not great but at the time it is annoying.

Directly the pain is felt, a good cure for it is to place the unfortunate finger upon the lower lobe of the ear, the soft lower end, in the manner shown in the sketch. Instant relief should be obtained.

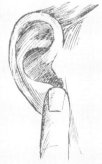

How to treat blisters

Many a ramble in the country has been spoilt by the appearance of a blister on the foot. The simple remedies are generally found to be the best, and in this case a remedy which is often beneficial is a cabbage-leaf.

A portion of the leaf should be cut to cover the painful part of the foot, and if possible stuck down with adhesive plaster. If the leaf is placed flat on the foot no difficulty will be experienced in putting on the stocking or shoe.

It is best to rest the foot for a little while after applying the cabbage-leaf cure, but in any case the pain is greatly reduced.

How to remove a splinter with a needle

Here is an excellent method of removing a splinter. Take a darning needle or bodkin and press the eye on the flesh around the splinter. The latter will come through the eye and can then be easily removed.

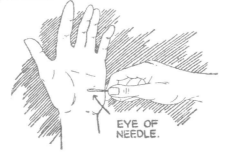

EYE OF NEEDLE.

Swimming made easy

It is not wise to go swimming on a completely empty stomach. If you must swim before breakfast, take a cup of cocoa and a biscuit. On the other hand you should never swim directly after a heavy meal. Wait at least an hour, and, if possible, two. If you break either of these two rules, you are liable to get cramp.

Losing presence of mind has undoubtedly been responsible for more deaths than the actual seizure

Overcoming Cramp

Undoubtedly this trouble, to which all swimmers are liable, is most unpleasant and dangerous. At the same time there is not so much danger in cramp as is generally supposed.

Losing presence of mind has undoubtedly been responsible for more deaths than the actual seizure.

If seized with cramp when near the shoreline lose no time in getting to land.

Remember that even should both legs be disabled you can paddle ashore with your hands. If both arms are seized, you have only to lie on your back and get to land by striking with your legs.

Should, however, assistance not be at hand, and the shore far away, different tactics must be adopted.

Should, however, assistance not be at hand, and the shore far away, different tactics must be adopted

First of all, retain your presence of mind!

If the cramp is felt in the calf of your leg, just below the knee – the most usual place – turn on your back at once, bend the toes upwards and kick out the affected leg in the air. You must ignore the pain, and paddle with one hand. With the other, rub the spot smartly.

Cramp in nearly all cases is due to indigestion, but it may be brought about by the low temperature of the water. Again, there are many persons who are always seized with it after having been in the water a little time. These will do well never to go out of their depth.

Care of scratches and small wounds

Any Scout who doesn't acquire his knowledge of hygiene from the old gossips knows that there is but one cause of blood poisoning – germ infection. Slight wounds or blisters or scratches are more likely to permit the entry of germs into the blood than are more severe injuries, because the latter bleed freely enough to wash out any germs which may have lodged in the wound at the instant of the injury.

If there is special reason to fear lockjaw infection, send for a doctor

The most effective bar to infection, in blisters, scratches, slight cuts or punctures of the skin is the immediate swabbing of the wound or skin with tincture of iodine. If there is special reason to fear lockjaw infection – and there should be if the tissues are crushed or badly soiled with street dirt or manure (which contains the lockjaw bacillus naturally), send for a doctor.

How to throw a lasso

Lasso throwing, though not largely practised by the English, is great fun. You require thirty feet of three-strand cord. Whip the ends, then wipe the rope over thoroughly with vaseline, letting it soak in well. Wipe off any surplus grease with a clean rag.

To use the rope, stand about ten paces from an upright post. Twirl the rope round your head several times, being careful to keep the casting loop open, and when it is spinning easily, let it out. If you are lucky it will settle round the post.

A great deal of time and patience is necessary if you wish to become an expert at lasso throwing.

Lasso throwing, though not largely practised by the English, is great fun

The art of lassoing

The art of lassoing, or roping, as we term it out West, is most deceiving. In theory it seems absurdly easy: in practice it proves far from easy.

The noose is made by tying a bow knot on a bight and passing the other end of the rope through the bight.

When the noose has been made – it should be about four feet in diameter – the slack of the rope is gathered up into smaller coils in the left hand. Then, taking care that the noose keeps open – for there lies the whole art of successful rope throwing – swing it around the head several times, and let it go as it comes to the front, past the right ear. The distance varies with the individual and also the object to be roped.

Sounds simple, doesn't it? And that's all there is in it; but if you really rope an object before you have practised several days, it will be something accomplished, I can tell you!

Be Handy

It's hard to picture him grouting the bathroom floor, but it was Napoleon Bonaparte who first said, "If you want something doing, do it yourself" (although he probably said it in French). Having the know-how and confidence to tackle simple practical tasks will stand you in good stead for life. Whether it's knowing how to build a bird box or how to hang a picture, you'll soon get a reputation for being reliable and efficient. The flip side is, this will mean lots more people calling on you for your help. But then that's what being a Scout is all about.

How to maintain your knives

To remove stains from knife blades, rub with a raw potato or thrust the blades into hard earth four or five times.

If you use a knife-board, warm it slightly before using. It will then give the knives a brighter polish. Always wipe knives directly after use, as this will save a lot of time spent cleaning.

When a knife becomes thin at the top have it filed off and the end rounded.

A smooth-faced brick is an excellent substitute for a steel, if you want a good keen edge on thin knives.

How to sharpen a saw

This is a job that should always be well done. Here is the best way to go about it.

Place the saw with the teeth upright on a flat, wooden surface and nail two pieces of wood on either side of the saw blade to hold it rigidly in position.

Then with a tapered, triangular-shaped file, shown on the right-hand side of the drawing, file the saw teeth – at a slight angle of about 30 degrees from each side – throughout its length.

The same angle must be maintained at each cut.

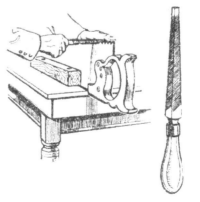

How to adjust a cistern-ball valve

Much expense may be saved when, with the simple knowledge required, household repairs can be done without the aid of a skilled workman.

The plumber, for instance, is usually called in to correct a flushing cistern which does not answer to the pull of the chain, when this fault can be remedied so easily by anyone.

The first sketch shows the ball valve. At the end of the hinged arm is a copper float which is raised by the rising water in the cistern until the needle valve, contained in the casting at the left of the sketch, shuts off the flow of water.

When, as in the next sketch, the water is shut off too quickly and does not rise high enough to permit the water to flush, the arm carrying the float should be bent upward until the correct level of water is obtained.

Similarly (see the third sketch), if the water rises too high and overflows, the float arm should be bent down until the required result is obtained.

This illustration shows the cistern-ball valve complete. On the left is the casting containing the needle valve, while on the right is the copper float.

a Water low – Bend up
b Water high – Bend down

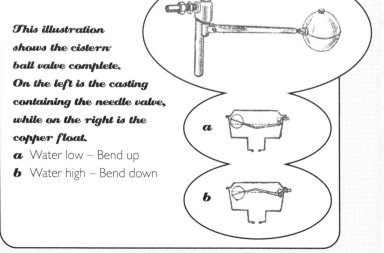

How to make Basuto sandals

You cannot very well walk about the streets in sandals, but they are jolly useful for clubroom or camp wear. This article tells you how to make them as the Basuto natives do.

The illustrations show the way the Basutos in South Africa make their sandals.

First of all you get a couple of pieces of leather just a little larger than your flat feet. Put your foot down on one and draw  round it with a pencil, taking great care to keep the pencil upright. Do not cut round this line, though. You must make the sandal half an inch bigger all round than your foot, so run another line round half an inch away from the other one, not with an ordinary knife, but with a 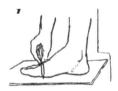 sharp knife, which makes all the difference. Diagram 1 makes this clear.

Now put your foot on the leather shape again and make a mark with a pencil between your big toe and the next one; then cut a little slit about half an inch wide across this mark, and two more slits parallel with the first one and about one-third of an inch apart. You will see what I mean from diagram 2.

After that you make the toe-piece (diagram 3a). It is better not to use leather which is too stiff or hard for this, because it has to fit snugly between the big toe and its neighbour. Use some soft fabric. You fix this toe-piece by putting the ends down through the first slit, up through the next, then down through the third slit; they are then made fast by putting the ends under their own standing points. Perhaps that is a bit

difficult to follow, but diagrams 3b and 3c will make it quite clear.

Having done all this, you next make the instep strap, which is simply a piece of stoutish leather about six inches long by one inch wide. Cut two half-inch slits in each end as shown in the fourth diagram.

Now put your foot in the sole again and mark the places on either side for the slits to take the instep strap. Again see diagram 2. Cut two one-inch slits and pass the strap through.

Then last of all make the retaining thong, which is a strip of rawhide, the stuff which merchants call Helvetia rawhide is best. You will want somewhere about two feet of it for each sandal, a quarter of an inch wide. If you examine diagram 6 carefully you will see how this is adjusted and made fast. Point each end of this thong, and just border the tips by toasting them by the fire a little. Bore three or four holes so that you can adjust the thong to any degree of tightness, and simply make fast by doubling the ends back on themselves and pushing the points through the hole which is most convenient. Diagram 6a shows the thong fastened.

Well, that is all there is in it, and having once worn sandals you will simply hate having to go back to boots. A great advantage of sandals is that you don't need to wear stockings with them; so there is no question of catching cold through wearing wet stockings in rainy weather; and also somebody – and I hope yourself – is saved hours of darning stockings or socks.

How to make a boot rack

Everyone should have a place in which to keep their boots, and a rack is just the thing for them. To make one, obtain two pieces of wood and cut them as shown.

Bore two holes in each, making them large enough to allow two wooden rods to be passed through as shown in the illustration.

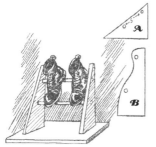

The length of the rods should vary in accordance with the number of boots the rack is to hold. Smear glue over the holes to keep the rods in position and then place the rack on a wooden tray or stand. Finish off with a coat of varnish.

If you want an artistic finish to the article, the side-pieces of the stand can be cut as shown by B.

"A" shows one side of the rack and indicates where the holes should be made; "B" illustrates how more elaborate designs could be made.

How to mend a kettle lid

Should the knob come off the lid of a kettle or pan, a new one can be put on in the following manner.

Slip a screw, head upwards, through the hole in the lid where the old handle was fastened, and fix a cork or small piece of wood on to the screw, as shown in the picture.

You will then have a handle as good as new.

How to join wire neatly

A very neat and effective join can be made by twisting the wires as shown in the illustrations.

The insulation should first be scraped from the wire and the latter bent as shown by "A". Both ends are then twisted as close together as possible. "B" shows the finished join.

Wireless enthusiasts will find this tip very useful.

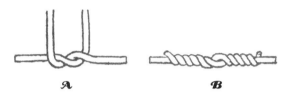

A   **B**

How to remove a tight screw

Anyone who has attempted to remove a very tight screw knows what a difficult business it is. After straining and twisting for a considerable time, the operator frequently ends by destroying the bite of the screw, which remains fixed as tightly as ever. With the aid of a pair of nippers, however, the affair is quite a simple one. Place the screwdriver in position, and then catch hold of the blade with the nippers just above the head of the screw. Press the screwdriver firmly, and at the same time twist round the blade with the nippers. The tightest screw will yield to this sort of persuasion.

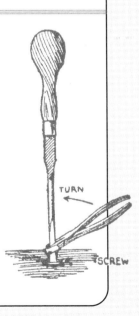

TURN

SCREW

How to keep cut flowers

If you are attending a sick person it is well to have some flowers in the room, and the following hints tell you how to preserve them.

When changing the water in which the flowers are standing, fill the vases with lukewarm water, adding a few drops of ammonia or lemonade to each vase. Flowers thus treated will last about a month.

If your patient has received any flowers through the post and they are faded, put their stalks into boiling water, which, if allowed to cool, will revive the flowers. Then cut off about two inches from the stalks and place the blooms in fresh water.

Always cut flowers in the early morning with a blunt knife, choosing the blooms that are only a little more than half in full blossom.

It is a good idea to arrange them in rain water which should, if possible, be renewed every day, with a little permanganate of potash and a pinch of common salt added.

Allow the flowers to keep all the foliage possible and throw away any slightly wilted blossoms. Cut a little of the stalks away every day.

How to make a weather vane

It is simple to construct, and effective in use.

Obtain a piece of tin and hammer it out flat. Now, take a pair of sharp scissors, and cut out the shape of a cock, arrow, or any figure you want, making certain that the tail half is larger than the head. You will also have to cut out four large letters: N–S–E–W.

When you have done this, obtain a small pole and saw a slit in it long enough to hold the vane. Bind the top with wire and point the other end of the pole. If possible, tip it with metal or a nail, and it will swing better.

You will now want a piece of beam, three or four inches thick. Bore a hole in one end, a little wider than the diameter of the pole. If the bottom of the pole is metal-tipped, put a small piece of tin into the hole, so that the pole can turn easily.

Bore two holes for the cross-rods, put them in, and nail on the letters. If you want to put the vane on a pole make another hole, as you see in the picture.

Make a V-shaped cut in the wood if you intend fastening it on to a roof, as shown also.

To finish, polish the pointed part of the pole with grease, and put some oil into the hole. Enamel or paint the vane, then set it up, taking care that "N" is pointing to the North.

How to make a post-box

Scouts often write letters at camp and put them in their pockets, only to forget to post them. The picture shows an easily made "gadget" which will serve as a post-box, to be cleared at regular intervals. Try one at your next camp.

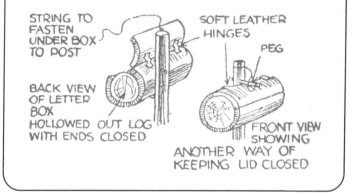

STRING TO FASTEN UNDER BOX TO POST

SOFT LEATHER HINGES

PEG

BACK VIEW OF LETTER BOX

HOLLOWED OUT LOG WITH ENDS CLOSED

FRONT VIEW SHOWING ANOTHER WAY OF KEEPING LID CLOSED

How to make simple hinges

STAPLE.

You can make two fine hinges for a gate out of the handle of an old pail.

Fasten two fairly strong staples into the gate-post. Now cut the bucket handle in two and open the ends wide enough to be hooked into the staples and closed again.

The cut ends of the handle are nailed to the gate as shown.

How to make a removable bird-house

If you possess a bird-house you have, no doubt, often experienced great difficulty when painting or redecorating it, as the house is generally screwed firmly to a pole from which it is almost impossible to remove it.

If you try this idea you will get over the difficulty quite easily. Cut down the top part of the post until it will fit into a disused tin. Make cuts and slots in this, as shown, and then nail it on to the underside of the bird-house, placing the other end over the pole.

Next take some strong nails and drive them through the slots and into the pole, as shown, bending their heads downwards so that the tin will be kept in a firm position.

If you wish to remove the house at any time, you just turn the nails to the position shown by the small right-hand sketch, and then the house will come away from the pole with ease.

How to oil a lock

The lock of a door often becomes stiff and prevents the door from shutting easily. A little oil may put things right.

In most locks there are tiny holes into which the oil is dropped, but if there are no such holes the oil can be applied with a feather. Dip the feather in sweet oil, and then insert it in the keyhole and twist it about. Next coat the projecting catch with oil and work the doorknob about so that the oil passes into the lock.

The suggestion of using a feather for oiling small parts of machinery is one worth remembering.

How to make a flower pot holder

Why not make a holder for Mother's flower pots?

Shape a piece of flat wood into a board large enough to take a flower pot comfortably. Then find a number of strips of wood

and make a framework as shown in the illustration.

Fit in the board at the bottom, and then fix four hooks in each top corner, through which pieces of cord are passed to enable you to hang up the holder.

You will, of course, construct the strips of wood according to the size of the flower pot.

How to make a weather-glass

A very reliable weather-glass can be made out of such simple materials as an empty salad oil bottle and a two-pound jam jar. Having procured these articles, pour sufficient water into the jar to cover the mouth of the bottle when the latter is inserted into the former as shown. In fine weather it will be found that the water will rise into the bottle, but will fall back into the jar again when wet weather is due. Though the idea of this quaint home-made barometer is not new, it is not generally known.

How to make a potato slicer

Whether at home or in camp, for quick frying, potatoes should be cut thinly.

This handy little hint will enable you to cut potatoes as thin as you please.

Obtain an old knife and at the top of it drill a hole large enough to take an inch and a quarter screw. Now place the screw through the hole in the knife and push the screw in the centre of the potato.

Holding the potato in one hand and the knife in the other, begin to slice the potato. You will find you can regulate the thickness you require and the knife will cut a continuous slice.

The knife will not be useless for other purposes because the hole will not interfere in any way.

How to build a plate rack

The only material required for making this plate rack is a suitable length of half-inch thick board and, should the width of the board described here not be available, the portion B could be made in two parts and fixed together in any suitable fashion.

A shows the size and shape of the two end pieces which are screwed to the back portion B as shown in F.

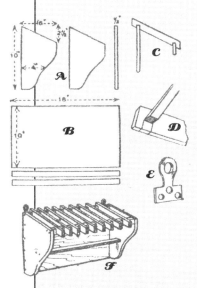

Two pieces of wood, the same length as B and about two inches wide, form the other horizontal supports for the end pieces F. The top one also acts as the bearer for the cross pieces between which the plates are inserted; whilst the lower one forms the base for the smaller plates which are not held by the top rail.

The cross bearers are cut as shown by the section in C, the sectional uprights representing the back portion and the top horizontal support.

D shows how the slots are cut in these bearers. Two saw cuts to a suitable depth cut the sides, whilst a chisel is used to complete the slot.

The suggested type of clip to be used is shown by E, though any type would do. These are screwed to the back board, as shown in F.

It will be seen that any number of cross bearers can be applied, and since they slide along the rails, plates and dishes of any size can be inserted.

How to hang a picture

To avoid damage and disaster, preparation is all. Dig out your power drill, wall plugs and screws. Think carefully about where you want to locate your picture – in line with your others, or artfully haphazard? The choice is yours.

Find a screw strong enough to take the weight of the picture and its frame. Match this to a drill bit and wall screw of commensurate size.

If drilling into a cavity wall, the most secure place is either a "stud" (vertical timber) or "nogging" (horizontal timber), which can be located by tapping a knuckle against the wall – a space will give a hollow sound, a timber less so.

Important: Do not drill below or above light switches or plug sockets; electronic testers are available which will confirm whether wiring is present behind the wall. If necessary, rethink the position of your picture.

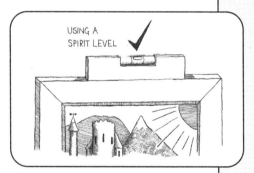

USING A
SPIRIT LEVEL

Once happy that you are drilling in a safe and secure place, drill a hole deep enough for the wall plug. Ensure the plug is snug and cannot move around in the hole. The screw should now work in easily with a hand-held screwdriver. Leave approximately one quarter of the screw proud from the wall on which to hang the picture on its string. Check the string has not perished, which you may find on older (and possibly more valuable) works of art.

Finally, use a spirit level to ensure it is hanging straight.

How to make a picture frame

The materials required to make a picture frame are very few.

A large variety of mouldings can be obtained at reasonable prices, so it is not worth while trying to make these. Mouldings of British and foreign manufacture are available, the latter being slightly cheaper, though not so durable, as the former.

A small 6 in. or 8 in. tenon-saw will be required, as also will a mitre box, the construction of which is explained here.

The first sketch shows the box itself and its use. It will be seen that it has three sides screwed together at the

base. The dimensions of the bottom side should be wide enough to allow for the widest moulding that will be used.

Across the centre make a careful saw-cut at an angle of 45 degrees down to the top of the base-board, from which it will be readily seen that a piece of moulding, marked to the correct length required and inserted in the box with the mark coinciding with the saw-cut, will be cut off at the required angle and to the correct length.

Care should be taken to see that the bevel is cut on the correct side of the moulding.

The next sketch shows the method of nailing the sides of the frame together, which, if the bevel is correct,

should be exactly at an angle of 90 degrees. The frame is now completed, and there now remains the framing of the picture.

After placing the picture in the groove of the moulding, cut a piece of cardboard – the same size as the picture – and place on top. This should bring its surface almost flush with the back of the moulding.

Hammer a suitable number of brads around the picture to hold it in its place (see the last sketch), then stick a piece of brown paper over the whole of the back, and finally trim up the edge.

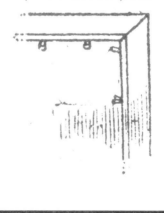

How to make a photograph stand

Photograph stands are always useful, and such articles generally find a ready market at bazaars and sales-of-work.

The stand illustrated is made from strips of wood, the length depending on the height or breadth of the photograph. The bottom cross-piece is screwed on from the front, and the top from the back as shown. The support is, of course, screwed on from the back. Round-headed, brass screws should be used, but the wood parts should be glued on first to ensure extra strength.

The support is hinged, and the extent of its opening is limited by a small chain.

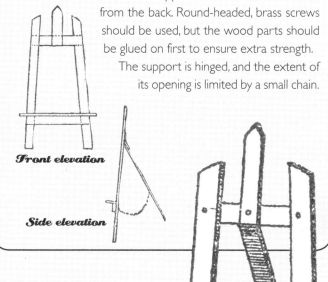

Front elevation

Side elevation

How to make a bedside table

You can make a useful bedside table from a wooden box, and a piece of wood which should be an inch wider all round than the ends of the box.

First plane off the rough surface of the box, then give it a good sand-papering inside and out.

Now purchase a bottle of varnish (dark brown stain), and colour the box, also the piece of wood which forms the table-top.

Screw the top to one of the ends of the box so that it overlaps evenly all round.

You can fix up a shelf or two inside the box; and a curtain hung over the front gives it a good finish.

How to mend broken leather

The sketches show an excellent way of joining two strips of leather. The first diagram illustrates the slit made at the end of one strip.

Notches are cut at the sides of the second piece of leather as in the next sketch. The ends are bent together, then slipped through the slit and pulled so that the notches fit tightly. The third sketch shows the finished join.

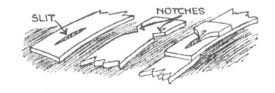

How to mend a broken caster

The first little sketch shows the broken and worn holes in which were the loose screws holding the caster to the bottom of the piece of furniture.

These holes must be made slightly larger with a reamer or any other handy tool, in order to receive the wooden pegs, shaped with a pocket knife or similar tool to fit the holes.

The next sketch shows how the pegs are driven into these holes; whilst in the third sketch the ends have been cut off ready

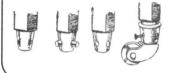

to receive the caster.

You are then shown the old screw replaced and the caster ready for use again.

How to make a string holder

Here is a handy string holder you can make. It will stand anywhere and will not overbalance when you pull the string.

A flat piece of wood about seven inches wide, ten inches long and three-quarters of an inch thick, forms the base. Two upright pieces of wood, ten inches long and half an inch wide, are fastened to each side of it and joined across the top by a

piece of wood half an inch wide by three inches long, in which has been drilled a hole large enough to take the string.

Now to the centre of the base of the holder an oblong, tapering piece of wood is fastened. To finish off the holder sand-paper it and give it a coat of varnish.

The ball of string should be placed on the centre piece of wood, the end of the string placed through the hole at the top of the holder, and your gadget is made.

How to make a wire egg holder

When an egg in taken out of the saucepan with a spoon, a quantity of water is also taken up, and when the egg is tipped on to a plate, the water goes too. This is not very pleasant and to prevent this you have to take hold of the egg with your fingers and no doubt burn yourself.

Here, however, is a good way to remedy this inconvenience and at the same time do a Good Turn to Mother.

Obtain a piece of thick wire (any metal will do) about twenty-eight inches long. Take a safety pin and study the bend at the end of it.

Now in the centre of the wire make a bend an inch in diameter on the same principle as the end of the safety pin. The sketch will give you the idea.

You can now shape the two ends in what ever manner you like and with the instrument that you have made, eggs can be conveniently lifted out of the boiling water.

Be
Presentable

From a job interview to a blind date, first impressions count. If your trousers are stained, your shirt is creased and your hair is a mess, then your chances of success are poor, no matter how charming or well qualified you happen to be. Even if your own manners and grooming are impeccable, try and be a little charitable to others less fortunate. A bestselling author, H. Jackson Brown, said: "Good manners sometimes means putting up with other people's bad manners."

How to greet the monarch

Contrary to popular belief, there are no hard or fast rules for greeting a king or queen. However, there are some traditional formal customs which many observe.

Men generally make a neck bow while women perform a short curtsey. A simple handshake is also considered quite acceptable. When it comes to speaking, you should treat the monarch as "Your Majesty," followed in subsequent exchanges by "Ma'am" or "Sir".

How to make a ready-made tie

If your necktie becomes creased and unshapely, you should make this little contrivance, which will help to keep it tidy and thus smarten your appearance.

Obtain a flexible arm-band and cut it in two, afterwards fixing the severed ends together with a hook and eye, or thin pieces of wire, hooked to form a clasp.

Now fix the tie on to the band with a permanent knot and then put it under the collar, as shown, when you wish to use it.

How to press your trousers

Everyone worth their salt presses their own trousers without troubling Mother; but you may find that, unless you already know this tip, the trousers will appear "shiny" after the operation.

This unpleasantness can be avoided by using a damp cloth as the fellow in the picture is doing, and ironing the trousers over this. The cloth, of course, should not be too damp.

When the trousers have been pressed give them an airing.

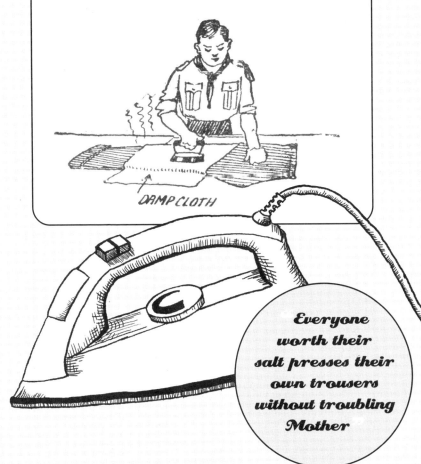

DAMP CLOTH

Everyone worth their salt presses their own trousers without troubling Mother

How to shave

There's nothing quite like a shave to help you freshen up or feel more handsome than you really are. If you are jet-lagged or otherwise jaded a shave is also the perfect tonic and can almost be as good as a sleep. While most chaps are shown by their fathers how to perform this daily ritual, many still don't know how to shave properly. Here's how.

Wash your face in warm, soapy water to eradicate dead skin cells and unwanted oils. The warm water will open your pores and make for a smoother shave.

Apply a shaving cream, gel or other lather to soften your hair and allow moisture into your skin. Shaving with conditioner is a fall-back position if none of the above is available and baby shampoo also works (if you are really stretched). Never shave without a lubricant as this will result in damage to your skin.

Hold your razor flat to your skin and angled at approximately 35 degrees. It can help if the skin is taut, so either pull the skin taut or puff out your cheeks to create a surface that is easy to shave. Then drag across the face, against the grain in a smooth, even and continuous stroke. Do not apply pressure to the razor or move it sideways. Do not go over the same area again – once should be enough if your razor is sharp; let the blade do the work.

How to remove grease spots

Grease spots are about the most unsightly stains that can deface a piece of cloth; one large grease spot will at once make a suit of clothes look shabby. There is, nevertheless, a simple and efficient way of removing grease spots. The material is laid upon an ironing board, and over the grease-mark is placed a piece of blotting-paper, or brown paper. Then a hot iron should be rubbed over the paper. In a few seconds the grease will be effectually transferred from the cloth to the paper. It is advisable to use several small pieces of paper during the operation, as the first piece is liable to become saturated, and is then incapable of absorbing all the grease.

How to remove grease stains from leather

A simple way of removing grease stains from leather articles is to coat the affected part with rubber solution such as is used for repairs to cycle tyres.

The edges of the stain should be moistened before the solution is applied and the latter should be allowed to remain on for a few minutes, after which it is peeled off. The rubber absorbs the grease, so that the stain will usually have vanished when the solution is removed.

How to brush your teeth

The main reason for cleaning our teeth, says John Furniss, is to reduce the daily build-up of bacteria. This film of bacteria is called 'plaque' and forms especially between and around the necks of our teeth. Much better to clean really well once daily than ineffectively two or three times a day.

1 Rinse first with a mouthful of water. This will help to get rid of food debris.

2 Use a tapered brush just wet with no toothpaste. Start the brush running on the outside of the top back teeth and gently apply five strokes around the neck of each tooth and five strokes between each tooth in turn (directing from gum margin to the tip of the tooth). Progressively 'walk' the tapered brush head around all the teeth in turn, outside and inner surfaces, upper and lowers.

Only apply very gentle pressure, let the brush do the work for you. You do not need to press hard with an electric toothbrush.

1. TAPERED BRUSH HEAD

2. ROUND BRUSH HEAD

3 Now change to a round brush head. Apply some toothpaste (ideally one containing fluoride) and carry out the same circuit around the teeth. This time 'cup' each tooth in turn, moving the brush from tip to the neck of each tooth, again first on the outsides and then on the inside surfaces. Apply more toothpaste into the round brush head as necessary.

4 You will now have a mouthful of toothpaste. Use this as a fluoride rinse. Keep your lips firmly together and 'pump' the toothpaste slurry around your mouth whilst counting up to 30.

Then carefully spit out into a mug. Do not, however, now rinse with water otherwise you will wash the fluoride off too quickly (needs four minutes ideally in tooth contact). Just leave it. If you look into your mouth five minutes later it will all have disappeared.

So there you have it. Good camping and good brushing.

How to be courteous

Politeness does not cost anything, and I hope all Scouts, at any rate, will try to practise it rather more than is usually done. It is all very well to be a "rough diamond", or to have a good heart beneath a surly exterior, but remember that it is the exterior that people see when they meet you for the first time.

A real man or woman is courteous; that is, showing deference, human sympathy and unbreakable good humour.

Here is a very important bit of courtesy that is too often forgotten, and that is to thank for any kindness you receive.

A present given to you is not yours until you have thanked for it.

Scouts and kindness are the same.

> *A present given to you is not yours until you have thanked for it*

Robert Baden-Powell

Chief Scout

How to prevent a sneeze

A sneeze is annoying at all times, but on some occasions it is liable to have very serious consequences. Suppose, for instance a Scout hiding in the bracken, or behind a tree stump, were to give vent to a sneeze, the hiding place would very soon be discovered. Therefore the following method of preventing a sneeze should prove useful to Scouts. When you find a sneeze coming on, and you can always feel it coming, place your finger on the upper lip, just under the nose, as shown in the illustration, and press gently. You will find this a certain cure for sneezing.

A sneeze is annoying at all times, but on some occasions it is liable to have very serious consequences

Squeaking boots

It is very annoying to find that your boots squeak. Squeaking boots can be easily cured in this way: from your shoemaker get two wooden pegs. Then, having made a small hole in the centre of the sole of each boot, drive the pegs home. After this you will find that your boots will squeak no more. This is a very much better plan than standing the boot in oil for a more or less lengthy period, the method which is usually suggested, for the oil not only discolours the boot, but makes it almost impossible to polish it for weeks afterwards.

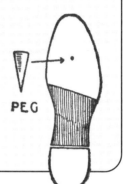

PEG

Keeping the tongue in place

When one's stocking or sock crumples up under the boot from being slightly too large, it creates a very unpleasant feeling. Similarly, when the tongue of one's boot persists in straying to the right or left, and doubles itself up, it becomes a source of great discomfort. But this is not all, the tongue loses its only reason for existence. Its position is between the opening necessitated for the lacing, and its purpose is to keep the moisture from reaching the foot in rainy weather, or prevent grit from entering the boot. Therefore the tongue should be kept in its proper place. To ensure it always being so, cut a small hole near the top and put one end of the lace through this before inserting it in the top lace-hole, in the manner shown in the diagram on the left. If this is done the tongue cannot shift from its position.

Walk upright

Have you a habit of stooping when walking? You have? Well, don't let it grow on you. You shouldn't slouch along as the fellow on the right is doing, either.

Try walking as you see the Rover on the left, with your arm behind you. This helps to keep your shoulders well back. Another good tip is to keep the head well up, so that the neck touches the back of the collar.

What size is your hat?

All hats do not have their sizes marked inside, and to those who are often at a loss as to the actual size of their headgear we give the following simple, yet accurate method of determining its size. Measure the width and length (as illustration), add the two together, and divide the total by 2. For example, the length may be 7⅜ and width 6⅛; the total of these two numbers when divided by 2 is 6⅞, the size of a hat of these dimensions.

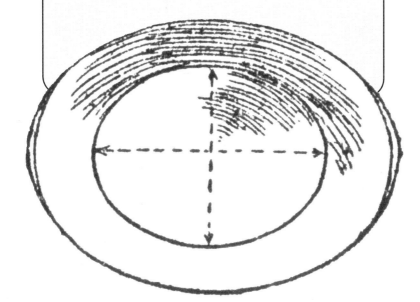

Be
Really Useful

Being useful isn't just about helping the elderly across roads. It's about being ready for any situation, from making a drinking cup to changing a nappy. You'll be just the sort of person everyone likes to have around. And there's a secret about helping people too – it makes you feel wonderful. It was none other than Mahatma Gandhi who said about volunteering: "The best way to find yourself is to lose yourself in the service of others."

How to change a nappy

Even if you are not a mother or father, this is an invaluable skill to learn. Parents of babies and toddlers are hard pressed at almost all times of the day and night and will appreciate a trusted friend or family member knowing how to assist in this most delicate of procedures. Be prepared to be an even more helpful uncle, aunt, niece or nephew. Despite their poor environmental credentials, almost all parents now use disposable nappies, which these instructions refer to.

Prepare your materials in advance. You will need a changing mat, wet wipes, disposable nappy and nappy sack. You may also wish to have cream or talcum powder to hand.

Carefully lay the baby flat on its back on the mat. Smile encouraging or speak gently to provide reassurance. Ensure the baby's head is comfortable.

Open the nappy sack in readiness for the wet or soiled nappy.

Remove the lower garments. If he or she is wearing a one-piece suit undo the lower buttons and move well above the waist. In one hand, gently raise the baby's legs together by holding the ankles or lower legs.

Undo the two tabs at the top of the nappy.

Quickly check the contents of the nappy to determine if wet or soiled.

If wet, simply remove and place into the open nappy sack. Use the wet wipe to clean the baby, paying special attention to the creases, which can become sore if left unattended.

If there is evidence of nappy rash (reddening) apply a little cream or talcum powder.

If soiled, use the nappy itself to capture as much of the waste as possible; using it like a flannel to scoop up the waste. Place in the nappy sack and only then use wet wipes to clean the remainder from the baby.

Quickly substitute a new, open nappy and place beneath the baby with the tabs at the top. This is to ensure clothing does not become wet or soiled mid change.

Once baby is clean, apply the cream or talcum power as above.

Bring the nappy together as if wrapping a parcel and secure the two sticky tabs inwards. Some parents also fold down the top of the nappy to prevent irritation to the belly button if this is still healing. Ensure the baby is content and that you have not applied the nappy too tightly or too loosely. If so, unstick the tabs and adjust the same nappy.

Place the used wet wipes into the nappy sack and double knot.

Re-dress the baby and check there are no damp patches on clothing. If any clothing is damp or soiled, it should be immediately replaced.

Dispose of the full nappy sack in a responsible way outside the house to prevent unpleasant odours.

Wash your hands and return the baby to its parent or activity.

"Laughter is like changing a baby's nappy," someone once said. "It doesn't permanently solve any problems, but it makes things more acceptable for a while."

How to volunteer

Want to feel warm and fuzzy without spending any money or having a drink in your hand? Then why not think about volunteering. It's about giving your time and skills for free. It seems to make no sense at all, but over 16 million people – almost a third of the UK population – volunteer on a regular basis and love it.

There are many reasons to volunteer: to give something back to your community, to use your skills or gain new ones. It's also a way to enhance your CV and improve your job prospects. But the main reasons people volunteer (according to research from The Scout Association) is for fun and friendship. Volunteering is a hobby with a purpose and an active social life. It's a new circle of friends and you go home knowing you have made a difference.

Most charities now offer flexible volunteering, which means that it can fit around your work, family and other commitments. You should be able to state the amount of time you have available, what skills you have and in which area you would like to work.

Two Ways to Volunteer

Visit www.do-it.org.uk – This is an inspiring and user-friendly website which connects potential volunteers with charities and other organisations. You type in the kind of volunteering you would like to do and your post code. It then brings up the opportunities available. Simple!

Visit www.scouts.org.uk – The Scout Association

offers fun, challenge and everyday adventure to 400,000 girls and boys across the UK. We have a positive impact on the lives of young people, our adult volunteers and our local communities.

Remember, volunteering should not be a chore – the right role for your time and skills should increase wellbeing, happiness and widen your social network. Everyone likes to feel valued and useful and volunteering is one of the best ways to achieve this. And you don't have to volunteer on your own either. Why not join with a friend and offer to help run a group together? Make volunteering your New Year's resolution. For example, why not think about volunteering instead of joining a gym – it will keep you fit, cost you less and is bound to be more fun than spending hours on the treadmill. Of course, as a volunteer, you might have a little less time left over to watch TV, but once you see the smiles on the faces of the people whose lives you have improved, you will never look back.

There are many reasons to volunteer: to give something back to your community, to use your skills or gain new ones

"Scouting is a character factory," says lead volunteer and Chief Scout, Bear Grylls. "We inspire a generation of young people to experience fun, friendship and real adventure. The opportunities to volunteer with us are flexible. Think of something you'd like to do and chances are it's just what we require. Scouting is about fun and friendship for adults too. And with more than 30,000 young people still on our waiting lists, there's no better time to get involved. You can give as much or as little time as you like."

How to tie knots for six different situations

Tie the following knots: reef knot, sheet bend, clove hitch, bowline, fisherman's and sheepshank and understand their special uses. The knots should always be made with rope, not with string. String is apt to slip round and alter the shape of the knot, but the knots, if properly tied with rope, will never slip. The tenderfoot should also be shown the practical use of the knots.

Before describing the knots and their uses, a short description of the composition of a rope may be found useful.

A rope is made out of a fibre called hemp. At a ropework the hemp fibre is first of all spun into what is called "yarn". The yarns are then spun together to make a "strand".

A hawser-laid rope is a rope made of three strands, laid what is called right-hand — that is to say, the strands run from left to right. This is the commonest kind of rope, and any Scout can see its composition by first unlaying the strands and then the yarns.

It is important to notice the "lay" of a rope when tying knots; don't tie a knot against the lay of the rope.

Three hawser-laid ropes, laid up together left-handed, form what is called a cable-laid rope.

So much for the ropes themselves; we will now consider how to tie the knots and their uses.

✱ A "bend" simply means a knot.

✱ "Bending" ropes means joining a rope to another rope or to a pole by a bend or hitch.

❊ A "bight" is a loop.

❊ A reef knot, sometimes called the sailor's square knot, is used for bending two dry ropes of the same size together. Used also in all "first aid" knots.

❊ A single-sheet bend is used for joining two dry ropes of different sizes together.

❊ For wet ropes, or in order to give greater security, a double-sheet bend is used.

A Reef Knot – The simplest of all knots, and is always used when a common tie is required. Its formation may be easily traced in Figs. 1, 2, 3. Having

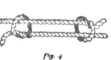

fig. 1   *fig. 2*   *fig. 3*

constructed the knot as far as Fig. 1, be sure part **a** is kept in front of part **b** as here shown, and the end **c** led in according to the direction of the dotted line.

Fisherman's Knot – Used to tie two wet lines or ropes together. A knot quickly made and easy to undo, the ends being simply pulled

fig. 4

apart. The diagram (Fig. 4) explains how this knot is made.

A Common Bend or Sheet Bend – In making a bend the ends of the two ropes are not used simultaneously as in forming a reef knot, but an eye or loop is first formed in the end of one of the ropes and the other rope's end is then rove through it in various ways, according to the bend desired. Fig. 5, single-sheet bend; Fig. 6, double-sheet bend, which gives greater security.

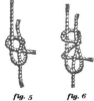

fig. 5   *fig. 6*

A Clove Hitch is used for securing a rope to a spar or pole. This hitch is always used for commencing and for finishing a lashing. A clove hitch is really a jamming form of two half hitches. Its formation is shown in three successive stages (Figs. 10, 11, 12).

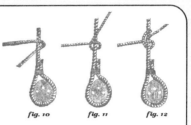

fig. 10   fig. 11   fig. 12

A Sheepshank – For strengthening a weak part in a rope, also used for shortening a rope. Gather up the amount desired

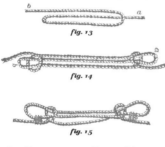

fig. 13

fig. 14

fig. 15

as in Fig. 13. Then with parts **a** and **b** form a half hitch round the two parts of the bight as in Fig. 14. To render it still more dependable, the bight **a** and **b** may be seized or toggled to the standing parts as in Fig. 15.

A Bowline – First taking part **z** in the right hand throw a loop over **c**, the end, as in Fig. 16. Secondly, lead **c** round behind part **a**, and pass it down through the last made loop, as indicated by the dotted line, and haul taut as in Fig. 17.

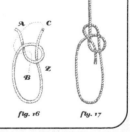

fig. 16   fig. 17

How to make a paper cup

Below is an easy way to make a handy drinking cup.

Take a piece of clean white paper 8.5 in. by 11 in., and fold in half as shown in Fig. 1, then diagonally as in the second figure.

The projecting corners are now turned over the edge of the cup.

Use good, strong paper as the strength of the cup depends on the quality used.

FINISHED CUP

How to carry cups

If you are ever asked to collect empty cups, don't make the mistake of placing them on top of each other in the manner shown on the left, because the least jolt will send them tumbling to the floor.

The correct way to hold them is shown in the other illustration, the handle of each cup touching opposite sides of the saucer.

wrong   *right*

How to make a drinking cup

Here's an idea for making a really jolly drinking cup – a noggin – which was described for the benefit of English Scouts by that grand old pioneer and backwoodsman, Dan Beard.

You know, or at any rate you ought to, that no self-respecting Scout goes about with axes and frypans and billycans hung about him like a pedlar's caravan. Just one thing is essential, and that is the knife; everything else should be in his rucksack except perhaps his noggin hanging ready for a drink if need be.

But How to Make It?

First of all you find a tree, for preference maple, beech or sycamore, which has, as you will find on so many trees, a little bump or swelling of the right size. Then you get permission to saw it off. If you live in town don't rush off to the nearest public park and start cutting the corns off the ornamental trees. There's no need to be an ass, and ask for trouble – you get plenty without asking.

The thing to do is just to keep this idea of

Decorate your staff with this brand: the sign for water

noggins in your mind until one day you are camping in the country and find a suitable tree with just the right bump – then get the owner's permission, and there you are.

Well, having done all this, saw off your knob of wood, as you see in the drawing opposite, and then get busy scooping out the wood in the middle until your cup is about an eighth of an inch thick; mind you don't go right through the shell – when you arrive at this stage you will find a certain amount of care is needed. Having got the shell thin enough, make it really smooth by using glasspaper. Then polish it with a little linseed oil and shellac well rubbed in.

If you are going to hang it on your belt, bore a hole and attach a strip of rawhide as you see in the diagram, fastening a small wooden toggle at the other end by a rawhide splice. To make this you simply cut two slits in the leather, slip the short end through the second slit and the long end through the first and haul taut. This will hold the rawhide absolutely securely, like the latigo lash.

When you have made your noggin decorate your staff with the brand illustrated by the title of this article. There's no need to tell you that it is the Native American sign for water.

When you have found the ideal "bump" on a suitable tree, saw it off.

Having done this, scoop out as much wood as you can, leaving the cup about $^{1}/_{8}$ of an inch thick.

To hang the cup to your belt, bore a hole in the wood, and attach by means of a piece of rawhide.

METHOD OF ATTACHMENT

To make the wooden "platter", get a piece of wood about a foot square.

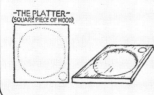
−THE PLATTER−
(SQUARE PIECE OF WOOD)

Scoop the wood from the centre. The small hole in the corner is for such things as salt.

How to open a bottle of champagne

When it comes to celebrating, for adults there's nothing quite like champagne. Before you think about opening it, however, make sure it's properly chilled. Around 7 degrees Celsius is perfect, which should feel very cold to the touch. Placing the bottle in a bucket of ice for 15 minutes will bring it to the correct temperature.

Aren't those corks annoying? Sometimes they won't budge despite all your efforts

Now dry the bottle, remove the foil and twist off the wire cage. Be warned, however – if the bottle has been shaken, the cork may now pop off of its own accord, so point the bottle away from yourself and others. Holding the bottle upright, place a towel over the cork.

Grip the cork firmly through the towel and place your thumb over the cork (just in case). Now here comes the important part. Grip the base of the bottle in your other hand and twist the bottle, not the cork. What you need is a soft pop – rather than a great explosion. Not only will this prevent cork marks on your ceiling, it will also preserve the bubbles in your champagne which are an essential part of the taste. Remove the towel and you should have kept every bit of your champagne in the bottle

Now it's time to pour, and the key word here is slowly. Pour just a little at a time (two fingers at the most), allow the bubbles to settle then repeat. When drinking, hold the glass by the stem rather than the bowl to prevent warming. Keep the rest of the bottle on ice.

How to remove a cork

Aren't those corks annoying? Sometimes they won't budge despite all your efforts. But perhaps you go about it in the wrong way.

For instance, if you are using a corkscrew, don't hold the bottle by the neck. You certainly won't get the cork out if you do. Get a firm grip on the body of the bottle as shown in the sketch, exert your strength and – pop! the job's done.

When opening a ginger-beer bottle which is liable to burst, cover it with a cloth. This will prevent possible injury.

Instead of cutting corks

After withdrawing a cork from a bottle the former rapidly expands, and when one wishes to replace it one frequently finds that it has become too large for the purpose.

The usual remedy in such cases is to pare pieces off the side. This, however, is seldom satisfactory, for the cork, as a rule, is far from airtight, and in some cases will not even keep the liquid in. A better way is to place it on the floor and roll it backwards and forwards with one's foot, putting a certain amount of pressure on it.

After a few minutes of this persuasive treatment it will have become fairly soft and can be inserted in the bottle without difficulty.

Be
the Life and Soul

We've all been to parties where no one appears to be having any fun. What they're missing is someone to break the ice, and having a few party tricks up your sleeve will help put people at their ease. You'll find one or two here – and once learned, never forgotten. The same is true for a day out. Football can become tedious after a while, so why not find out how to make your own kite? It's the nearest you'll get to flying with both feet still on the ground. People will remember you for your resourcefulness and upbeat outlook. As Bear Grylls has said, "Always try and be the most positive person in the room."

How to choose the right size bottle

There are all manner of weird and wonderful terms for classifying the myriad objects in the world. One of the more eccentric systems is the use of the names of Old Testament prophets and kings for wine bottles. What would they have made of it all!

Quarter bottle – Split or Piccolo (187.5 or 200 ml)
Half bottle – Demi (375 ml)
Bottle – Imperial (750 ml)
Magnum (1.5 litre) 2 bottles
Jeroboam (3 litre) 4 bottles
Rehoboam (4.5 litre) 6 bottles
Methuselah (6 litre) 8 bottles
Salmanazar (9 litre) 12 bottles
Balthazar (12 litre) 16 bottles
Nebuchadnezzar (15 litre) 20 bottles
Melchior (18 litre) 24 bottles
Solomon (25 litre) 33.3 bottles
Primat (27 litre) 36 bottles
Melchizedek (30 litre) 40 bottles

For your next concert

Here are a few hints for your next concert:

- The "chuff-chuff" of a train can be represented by the rubbing together of two pieces of glass-paper; the sound of breaking windows by flinging small pieces of brass on the stage behind the scenes, so that a tinkling noise is produced.
- For a reproduction of falling crockery, small pieces of china should be passed from one basket to another.
- A gramophone is very useful at a concert.
- Peas rattled in a sieve make a good imitation of falling rain.

How to make money

First half fill a glass tumbler with water, then throw a bright 10 pence piece into the water and cover the glass with a plate. Now reverse the whole lot, and turn the glass round rapidly.

The 10 pence piece will now be seen gleaming on the plate, and a second coin will appear to be swimming on the surface of the water.

It is a refraction of the rays of light which causes this curious illusion.

The moment the glass is restored to its original position, and the water ceases to move, the second coin disappears.

This trick can easily be performed without spilling water, but to avoid accidents don't perform the trick above anything that might spoil.

How to pull a cake out of a hat

Breaking an egg and pouring the contents into a hat wouldn't do the latter much good, would it? This simple trick shows you how it can be done without injuring the hat.

This is the sort of trick that never fails to go down well. The magician borrows a hat, preferably a bowler, from a gentleman in the audience, breaks an egg on to a plate, pours it into the hat, and finally produces a cake by holding the hat for a moment over the flame of a candle. The hat is then returned to its owner, none the worse for its unusual experience.

How it is done – The whole secret lies in the cake. Procure a cake of the round variety, small enough to drop easily into a hat. Hollow out a space in the bottom of the cake, and push into this space an ordinary glass "unspillable" ink-well of the largest size you can get. A sectional view of the "faked" cake is shown in the illustration.

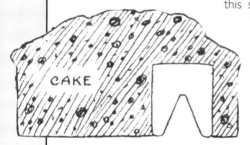

Place this cake on the bottom of a large plate, and stand the plate on a chair, on its edge and leaning against the back of the chair, in this way the cake is concealed behind the plate.

Borrow the hat, pick up the plate and place it over the mouth of the hat. Of course, the cake is picked up behind the plate, and drops unseen into the hat. The cake will fall with the bottom uppermost.

Break the egg, which must be a small one, on to the plate, beat it up with a fork, add a pinch of flour, etc., and then pour the mixture into the hat. The liquid will run into the ink-well, and any that may be spilt will naturally soak into the cake, so that the hat is quite safe from harm.

Replace the plate on the hat, but upside down this time, and hold it for a moment over the flame of a candle, taking care not to scorch the hat.

After making yourself busy in this way, turn the hat over and remove the plate with the cake upon it. The liquid will not run out, owing to the ink-well's construction, and if it has been placed near the edge of the cake, slices may be cut from the cake and handed round to the audience. This is a very convincing finish to the trick, and one which never fails to go down well, in more ways than one.

How to do a party trick

How to Balance Pennies Between your Fingers

This is a neat little trick which, although it looks quite simple, is really rather difficult.

What you have to do is to hold four pennies between all your fingers and your thumb in the manner shown in the sketch. It will become quite simple after you have tried a few times, but a lot of fun can be obtained from it if two players start to do the trick simultaneously with four pennies.

The winner will, of course, be the player who gets all four coins between his fingers and thumb first and holds them aloft without a spill. Do not, however, attempt to hurry over this trick or you will drop the whole lot.

How to make a kite

Getting Fun from Windy Weather

First of all you must obtain a piece of wood about three feet long and half an inch wide. Sticks used in the garden to act as supports for plants will do splendidly – but ask permission to take one first!

Now you will want a piece of flexible cane. This is bound with strong, light twine at the top of your piece of wood, just below A. The ends of the cane – C and D – are bent, and tied together firmly with string, so that a semi-circle is formed of the bent cane and the string.

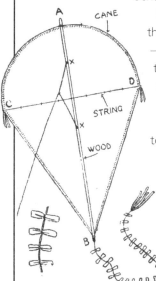

Now take more string and connect the cane at C to the foot of the wood – B, then take your string up to D and tie firmly. Little tassels at C and D will help your kite when it is ready for flight.

Now ask for some calico – enough to cover the kite frame (calico is a plain, tough cotton cloth). Lay the frame on the material and cut all round, but not too close, as you must allow for the edges of the calico to be sewn to the frame.

When the calico is sewn to the frame, bore two holes through AB as shown by the crosses just above and below the line CD. Now pass a piece of fine string through the two holes, allowing it to protrude in front of the calico.

Make a number of knots in each end of the string so that it will not pull through the holes, for the strain of your flying line [

will be on this string. The illustration shows how the flying line is fixed.

The only thing to be done now is to make the tail. This is very simple indeed. Fold small pieces of paper and tie them in the centre with string, until you have a long chain. About thirty-five papers and a tassel should be used.

Along comes a nice breezy day! Ask your chum to go into the park to help you. Get him to hold up the kite for a moment. Run forward, and let the kite run into the wind.

If it does not go up easily, but "bumps" in the air and comes down tail first, then the tail is too long. Take off a few papers.

If the tail is not long enough, the kite will dive downwards.

A little alteration, and you will then have a kite capable of flying many feet above the highest trees in the park.

Kite making: sticks used in the garden to act as supports for plants will do splendidly – but ask permission to take one first!

How to make a cake

A Victoria Sponge is one of life's great treats. It is not only a wonderful way to brighten up a dull afternoon, it is great activity to do with children, and you can eat the results.

There are many schools of thought when it comes to cake making but also surprisingly strict rules when it comes to the Victoria Sponge itself. Enjoyed and made popular by Queen Victoria (1819–1901), a genuine Victoria Sponge must be filled with whipped cream and raspberry jam and finished with a dusting of icing sugar (or, controversially, caster sugar according to the Women's Institute). Here is the fail-safe method.

Ingredients

For the cake
3 large eggs
6 oz self-raising flour
6 oz caster sugar
6 oz soft butter
A teaspoon of baking powder
A capful of vanilla essence
For the filling
Double cream, whipped
Good quality raspberry jam
For the topping
Icing sugar or caster sugar

Preheat the oven to 180°C/fan oven 160°C/gas mark 4.

Grease two cake tins with butter.

Mix the eggs, flour, sugar, butter and baking powder in a bowl, remembering to double sift the flour – this is vital in achieving a light and fluffy consistency. Beat the ingredients, but do not overbeat as this will remove the air from the mixture and prevent the cake from rising. Add the vanilla essence and stir well.

Divide the mixture evenly between the two tins and transfer to the oven.

Cook for 27 minutes in a fan assisted oven, or 30 in a conventional oven.

Remove and allow to cool before removing from the tins; if you try and remove too early the cake will stick and break apart.

Allow the cake to cool fully before adding the whipped cream and jam sandwich filling.

Dust lightly with sugar and serve on a doily with Earl Grey, Ceylon or Darjeeling tea.

A LIGHT DUSTING OF ICING SUGAR

SPONGE CAKE

WHIPPED DOUBLE CREAM

GOOD QUALITY RASPBERRY JAM

A DOILY

A CUP OF EARL GREY, CEYLON OR DARJEELING TEA

A twirling penny

Here is an amusing trick to practise on your chums.

What they have to do is to try to pick up a coin from a table 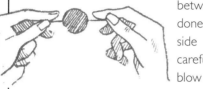 between two pins. This can be done by placing a pin on either side of the coin. You then carefully lift the coin up and blow on it.

The penny will then twirl round at a fast rate, and it is fun to see who can keep this up the longest, but it is not so easy as it seems.

The whole secret of the trick is that the two pins must be in direct line with one another but, of course, you don't want to tell your chums that, until they have dropped the coin several times.

A smart trick

Here is a catch which will mystify your pal every time.

Put twenty-one matches on the table. Now explain to a friend that the idea of the game is for each player to draw any number of matches up to three from the pile in turn. The one who draws the last match is the loser.

You invite your pal to draw first. If he draws one match, you draw three, and so on, in order to make a total of four for the two draws in every case. If you do this each time, your friend will always find himself with the last match!

Where are you wounded?

Here is an excellent little game. Scatter the players, one being in the middle whose object is to touch anybody. The person touched then becomes "centre person" and, placing his or her hand wherever they were touched (wounded), they try to touch somebody else.

Obviously the centre person should try to touch another player so that on becoming centre person they find it difficult to run owing to the fact that they have to hold their hand on the place touched. A most difficult place is the ankle, as shown in the illustration.

"Scout's nose"

Here is an excellent game to play while indoors. You should try it next time things are a little dull at the clubroom.

Prepare a number of paper bags, all alike, and put in each a different smelling article, such as chopped onion in one, coffee in another, rose-leaves, leather, orange peel and so on.

Put these packets in a row a couple of feet apart, and let the competitors walk down the line and have five seconds' sniff at each.

At the end of that time they have one minute in which to write down or state the names of the different objects they have smelt – in their correct order.

This game is a splendid test for your sense of smell.

Be Smart

There are certain skills that just have to be learnt. Whether it's how to remember things, how to write a poem or how to tell the age of birds, your friends will be astonished at your abilities. And because the modern world can sometimes be baffling, expensive and frustrating, you have to have your wits about you. Knowing the right and wrong ways of doing things will always stand you in good stead, from how to get a job to how to vote. And knowing something others don't is always fun too. But no matter how smart you feel you are, people will always judge you by what you do, rather than what you know. It was Napoleon Hill who said, "Action is the real measure of intelligence."

How to calculate the height of a tree

All Scouts should be able to judge height. Here is a method by which the approximate height of a tree can be easily discovered. Two well-planed pieces of wood are procured and fastened together at an angle of forty-five degrees. A thick piece of wood is also prepared for use as a post, and the angle is placed on this so that the base of the angle A is perfectly parallel with the ground.

A sight is then taken along the line B, and the stand is next moved forward or backward until the top of the tree comes within the line of sight. The measurement is taken from the spot C, where the imaginary line would reach the ground, to the foot of the trunk of the tree, and the figure thus obtained represents approximately the height of the tree. The more level the ground the more accurate will be the estimate.

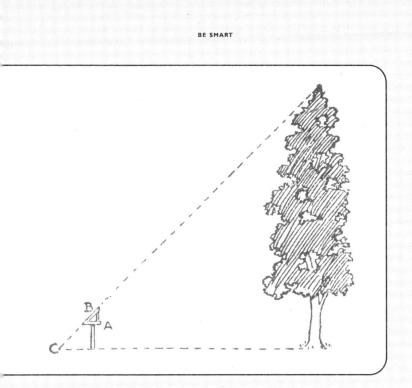

How to measure the speed of a train

All observant Scouts when travelling by rail are interested in knowing at what rate the train is going. Here is a paragraph by which you will be able to tell the speed at which you are travelling when you are in the train. Little posts are placed at every quarter of a mile distant along the line; marked ¼, ½, ¾ or a whole number. They are of great help to the engine-driver, as by their aid he can regulate his speed. The numbers signify the distance from the particular spot to the London terminus. By counting the number of seconds between these posts and dividing 900 by the sum, you will get the speed of the train.

How to make a simple electrical switch

When next you are "stunting" with electricity, make the switch illustrated in the sketch.

Two Meccano strips with a flat bracket are taken and fixed to the board or such like, with the aid of screws. The two

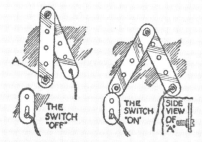

electrical wires are fastened to the strips and bracket as illustrated in the first sketch.

A screw is fitted to the last hole of the first strip for use as a handle, and all you have to do to form a circuit is to connect this strip with the bracket.

These parts can be made quite easily from tin, if you haven't a Meccano set, or the odd Meccano parts can be purchased for a few pence from local dealers.

How to notice things

Nothing is too small or insignificant to be noted.

Birds rising suddenly and circling in the air denote the approach of someone.

The ashes of a fire should be examined; if warm, the person who made it is not far away.

Note carefully every change in direction you take.

When examining a river, note its direction, rapidity, where fordable, height of banks and bridges.

Always notice all peculiar features and landmarks while going over strange ground, especially by frequently looking backwards so that you may be able to find your way back again by them. One pair of trained eyes is as good as a dozen pairs untrained.

Observation and deduction are the basis of all knowledge. The importance of the power of observation and deduction to the young citizen can therefore not be overestimated. Children are proverbially quick in observation, but it dies out as they grow older, largely because first experiences catch their attention, which they fail to do on repetition.

Scouts have not only got to see everything, but use their ears and nose and hands. Above all, Scouts have got to use their minds, so that they can think out the meaning of the things they notice.

Let nothing be too small for your notice: a button, a match, a hair, a cigar ash, a feather or a leaf might be of great importance.

If you are in the country, you should notice landmarks, that is, objects which help you to find your way or prevent you getting lost. Notice distant hills and church towers; and nearer objects such as peculiar buildings, trees, gates, rocks etc. You may want to use your knowledge of them some day for telling someone else how to find his way. You must notice and remember every by-road and footpath. Remembrance of these things will help you to find your way by night or in fog when other people are losing themselves.

By night, of course, you must use your ears instead of your eyes, and practice at this helps to make perfect.

How to sketch

Scouts who sketch from nature will find this contrivance a great help. It consists of a frame, with your drawing-paper pinned on one side, with a glass at right angles to it, with equal spaces marked on it. You look through this at your landscape, and it is much easier to get the right proportion, because your paper is also divided in equal parts. A convenient size is ten inches by seven inch sight measure.

How to remember things

With so much going on in our heads, it's a wonder we can remember our own name. The good news is that there are a number of tricks you can use to help you remember sequences of information.

Mnemonics

The most common solution is to come up with a mnemonic – a memorable sentence that contains information about something else. For example: Richard of York Gave Battle in Vain is a mnemonic to remember the colours of the rainbow in the right sequence: red, orange, yellow, green, blue, indigo and violet.

How to write a poem

Don Paterson once described a poem as "a little machine for remembering itself". Like a finely crafted watch, all of the poem's components need to be working perfectly in tune with each other.

Your most important component is your idea. This is the fuel cell that will power your poem; if it's a fine idea, the poem should almost write itself; it will be bright and illuminating and fire you with all sort of other ideas and possibilities. You should have lines to spare by the end. If it's weak, your poem will be dim; it will fizzle out before you've even started.

William Shakespeare's famous Sonnet 18 is an excellent case in point. The poem is built around a central simile (comparison) – the idea of a summer's day. This comparison offers all sorts of possibilities and allows the poet to wax lyrical about "darling buds of May" and so forth.

Shall I compare thee to a summer's day?
Thou art more lovely and more temperate.
Rough winds do shake the darling buds of May,
And summer's lease hath all too short a date.
Sometime too hot the eye of heaven shines,
And often is his gold complexion dimmed;
And every fair from fair sometime declines,
By chance, or nature's changing course, untrimmed;
But thy eternal summer shall not fade,
Nor lose possession of that fair thou ow'st,
Nor shall death brag thou wand'rest in his shade,
When in eternal lines to time thou grow'st.
So long as men can breathe, or eyes can see,
So long lives this, and this gives life to thee.

However, what makes the poem brilliant is that the comparison is subsequently withdrawn and deemed inadequate. A summer's day can be uncomfortably hot, it can cloud over, it suffers from rough winds and by its very definition, it ends. It is not a suitable simile for his lover's "eternal summer". Across its fourteen brief lines, it involves the reader in the construction of the poem, and the poet's thought process. This is what gives the poem an engaging "voice" – you are for a moment in the poet's mind (and being Shakespeare's what more fascinating place to visit?). In a sense of course, he is showing off – proving he could write the poem any number of ways.

To begin, you need certain raw materials: pencil, paper, peace and quiet. The best poems are emotion recollected in tranquillity, not written in the heat of the moment.

Choose your idea; this could come to you in a flash of inspiration. If you're short of inspiration, why not visit a museum, art gallery or perhaps imagine a famous person in a strange place or situation.

Choose your form. This could be a fourteen-line sonnet, like Shakespeare's. A sonnet has a formal turn at line eight. It begins with eight lines of description; it concludes with six lines of reflection. It's very concise; every line has to earn its place and it encourages you to think as well as describe. It is also brief. A good poem should not outstay its welcome.

Come up with a brilliant first line. Not as easy as it sounds; but try this. Just write down as many lines as you can based on your idea, and in any order. After half an hour or so, look back on your work. With a bit of luck, one line will stand out from the others – more striking, more evocative, memorable or unusual than the rest. This should be your first line.

Read your poem aloud. As you write, read little pieces aloud. If it sounds wrong, it probably is wrong. It should canter along, not sound stumbling and halting (unless you specifically want it to). The sound should reflect the meaning. Use repeated vowel sounds (assonance) to add depth and space; use repeated "s" sounds (sibilance) to echo the wind or to represent the sound of the sea.

Develop your theme; take your idea for a walk and see where it leads. Don't be afraid to "explode the idea" and go in slightly silly or outrageous directions – you can always cross it out. What have you got to lose?

Use all five senses in the poem – make the poem come alive so the reader can smell, touch and feel what is going on. Don't just take a photograph with words. If it's a poem about a wood on a snowy morning, put the reader in the wood. Let them hear the squeak of the snow beneath their boots. When Shakespeare's Darling Buds of May shake in the wind, you can hear the rustling of the branches. When he talks about "too hot the eye of heaven shines" you can feel the heat on your face.

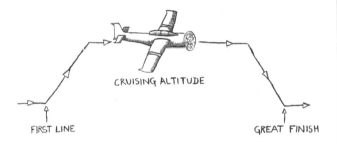

CRUISING ALTITUDE

FIRST LINE   GREAT FINISH

Have a great finish. The poet Paul Muldoon talks about a poem as if it's an aeroplane. Your first line is your take off; it then reaches cruising altitude then you have to bring it in to land, which can be hardest part.

You might not be writing Wordworth's "Daffodils" or "Sonnet 18" at your first attempt, but by following these rules you should have a very tidy piece of writing. Then share it with your friends; develop a thick skin and keep writing!

How to tell the age of birds

To many people each bird in a flock of sparrows appears to be exactly like its companions; but in reality the difference in their ages is fairly apparent to the close observer.

The sparrow in the prime of its little life displays a smooth coat of feathers and a coloured head which soon turns into a ruffled mass of drab grey.

The "caw" of a young rook is a high-pitched, uncertain noise – very different from the steady rasp of the older bird, while its flight is also very uncertain.

The heads and claws of younger birds are almost invariably out of proportion to the body, and they have considerable difficulty in balancing on a twig after alighting.

The young starling is a plain brown bird lacking the shiny coat of its parents.

How to tell the age of fish

It is quite natural to imagine that the age of a fish would correspond with its weight and size. Actually, however, this is not the case.

To find the age of a fish you must examine its scales and look for the tiny rings on each which indicate a year's growth, much in the same way that a tree's rings denote age.

The reason why the rings on the scales are not evenly spaced is because when food is plentiful, the fish grows more rapidly than during the lean times.

How to make a hectograph

We are repeatedly receiving enquiries for particulars of how to make a medium for reproducing handwriting in quantities.

Procure a biscuit tin lid, which should be tested to see that it is water-tight.

Obtain 1 lb ordinary gelatine. Put it in a saucepan, cover it with water, and boil until it has melted. Then add two teaspoonfuls of glycerine, and stir the mixture well.

Place the biscuit tin lid on a flat table, and pour the mixture into it, being sure that it is perfectly level before allowing it to set.

The copying is quite easy. With a gilt pen and aniline ink write out your copy, rather thickly, but in a clear hand. Then wipe the composition with a damp flannel.

Lay your copy face downwards on the composition, and press firmly and smoothly.

Do not touch it for about two minutes, in which time the writing should be transferred. You can then print off copies – laying each one on the composition and pressing firmly upon it. Take off the paper carefully.

To remove the writing, wipe the composition with the flannel, rubbing one way only; then leave it for a few hours.

How to text for free

Almost from the moment SMS (Short Messaging Service) was born, texting became the preferred method of communication. Ideal for simple messages, jokes and comments, it's somewhere between a phone call and an email.

But phone companies know how much we love to text too. The price of data services is rising, making texting less of an easy option. However, no sooner does a problem present itself than the digital community responds with a solution. Here are several ways to text for free, including some old Scout favourites.

BlackBerry Messenger – Although this is principally a BlackBerry-to-BlackBerry service, you can communicate with other people by adding your pals to the BBM friends list.

iMessage – This is a free unlimited text message service for all users of iOS 5 with Wi-Fi or 3G. It can be used between those who have an iPad, iPhone, or iPod Touch.

Text Free – Android users need not fret; there is something for you too. Download this from Google Play.

Google Voice – Another option available for Nokia S60, BlackBerry, Android and iPhone.

Semaphore – Learn this simple language and send messages up to a distance of half a mile. See page 149 to learn the alphabet.

Smoke signal – Used for centuries by the Greeks, Chinese and Native Americans smoke can be used to communicate in some circumstances. Many different systems have been used over the years – so why not devise your own? Ensure fires are kept under proper control and that you have the landowner's permission to make one.

Message in a bottle – If you're not concerned about getting a quick reply, then why not consider a message in a bottle? Originally used to demonstrate the flow of sea and ocean currents, it is the preferred messaging service of the castaway. The longest recorded delay is ninety-two years from writing to delivery. Think about that the next time your text message is delayed!

How to press flowers

The old-fashioned method of pressing flowers, leaves and such like, is to place them between the leaves of a book; but this often destroys many of the more delicate markings on the foliage, and so is not recommended.

A better plan is to place the specimens between two sheets of blotting paper, and on top of this lay a bag containing dry sand. The bag should not be more than three quarters of an inch thick when pressed out flat.

About a fortnight's pressure under the bag will be sufficient for average specimens, but some tough varieties may need rather more. Specimens treated in this way can afterwards be mounted in scrap albums by means of strips of adhesive paper.

How to get a job

It sounds obvious, but only apply for jobs that you actually want. Your interest (or lack of interest) for the work will show through in both your application and interview. Here are some tips to help you land the perfect situation.

If the employer asks you to submit a CV, keep it short and relevant, putting your most recent, pertinent experience first. A concise, well written two- or three-page CV will be a refreshing change for most employers. Avoid fancy fonts and above all make sure there are no typos. Ask a friend to proofread it for you.

If you get an interview, do your homework beforehand; the potential employer will want to know that you are interested in their company or organisation. Look at the website and annual report and mention something relevant during the interview. Do not bring up any personal information you have discovered about the interviewers; this is stalking behaviour!

Remember the interview is a conversation, not an interrogation. In a sense you are also interviewing your potential employer. Be relaxed, but not too relaxed. Dress smartly, but not in something so smart you feel uncomfortable.

Check yourself in a mirror immediately before the interview for food on your face or teeth or items of clothing that may have gone awry. You will be mortified to find out that your collar was turned up the whole time. It's best to decline offers of biscuits and tea; this is only to invite disaster. A glass of water should be fine.

A firm handshake and maintaining eye contact will help establish trust and rapport.

Always try and illustrate your answers with relevant examples from previous employment or work experience. People are much more interested in real situations.

Prepare examples of challenging situations that have arisen through no fault of your own, and explain how you steered them away from disaster. This should show your initiative, team working and leadership skills. Otherwise, avoid dwelling on things that have gone wrong; it could sound negative.

> *A firm handshake and maintaining eye contact will help establish trust and rapport*

At the end of the interview, ask a great question such as "what's the best thing about working here?" As well as providing useful information, it will turn the tables on the interviewer and take the pressure off you. Avoid lots of questions about salary and holidays. They want to know you are interested in the work, not just the benefits. Above all, do not have a very long list of questions; this is likely to bore the interviewer.

Believe in yourself; you're worth it!

How to vote

It's easy to take democracy for granted. The right to vote independently is one of our great freedoms and yet many people do not exercise their right simply because they don't know how.

Democracy is a Greek term meaning "rule by the people" – it therefore cannot exist without the co-operation of citizens like you. It is generally accepted as the fairest and most civilised system to determine the governance for a state. Apathy and ignorance are democracy's great enemies, so don't fall victim to either. "The ignorance of one voter in a democracy," said John F. Kennedy, "impairs the security of all."

Make sure you are on the electoral register. You can check this by calling your local council. You will then receive a poll card through the post.

Visit the polling station where you will cast your vote. This will be indicated on your card. This is often a school, church hall or community centre and it will be open usually from 7am to 10pm.

Give your name and address to the person at the desk; they will cross reference this with the electoral register. You do not need your poll card to vote, and this will not be used in the voting process.

You will be provided with a ballot paper containing a list of the parties and candidates.

Take this into the polling booth and read the instructions. You will normally be asked to put a cross by the name of your preferred party or candidate. Do not write your name, a comment or anything else on the paper or your vote will be "spoilt" and will be discounted.

Fold your ballot paper and drop it into the ballot box.

Above all, your vote should be secret and your personal

choice; do not tell the officer or any other person who you intend to vote for and do not be bullied into voting for someone you do not support.

Other Ways to Vote

By post – vote from the comfort of your own armchair by filling in a postal vote application form; this can be obtained from www.aboutmyvote.co.uk

Voting by proxy – if you are unable to go to a polling station, you can authorise a friend or family member to do this on your behalf. Fill in an application form from www.aboutmyvote.co.uk Reasons to vote by proxy could be because you have a disability, you are on holiday at the time of the election, you live or serve overseas or because you have an unavoidable work commitment.

For either of these alternative options, ensure you give the authorities plenty of notice (at least a month before the election is sensible). There's no excuse not to vote.

How to walk on the right side of a lady

Never forget to be courteous when accompanying a lady. Always walk with her on your left so that your right hand is free to guard against any danger. When, however, the kerb of the pavement or the edge of the path is on your left, you must break the above rule and walk on the side nearest the road.

What's Wrong?

How to write an invisible message (1)

The following is a novel and not very well-known method of writing a dispatch in such a manner that it appears to be a piece of blank paper to those who are not in on the secret. You must first soak your paper in water and place it on a sheet of glass. Then laying a sheet of dry paper over it write your message on this with a blunt pencil. Let your paper dry, and entrust it to the dispatch bearer. Your friends on receiving the blank paper will have to immerse it in water before they can read the message.

Imagine the discomfort of an enemy who, having captured the dispatch after much labour, finds what seems to be only a piece of blank paper. A caution is necessary. Do not dry your paper before a fire or over a lamp.

How to write an invisible message (2)

Here is a new method of preparing invisible writing. Clean the nib of the pen well before using and then dip it into a glass of clear water, and write your message on paper with the water.

When the words are quite dry spread ink over the surface of the paper and your message will appear quite clearly. Remember to allow the water to dry naturally, not before a fire or lamp.

How to know your flag

The Union Jack is the national flag of the United Kingdom and is made up of the old national flags of the former three kingdoms. In 1606 King James VI of Scotland and I of England added to the flag of Scotland (which was a blue flag with the white diagonal cross of St. Andrew), a red cross with a white border to represent the flag of England (which was a white flag with the red cross of St. George). Thus the Scottish and English flags were blended to form the first British Union flag.

In 1801 a red diagonal cross with a white border, representing the white flag with the red cross of St. Patrick of Ireland, was added to the flag, making the Union Jack of Great Britain and Ireland as we know it today.

Scouts must understand the right and the wrong way of flying the Union Jack. If it is flown upside down it is a signal of distress.

It will be noticed that the red diagonal arms of the flag have white bands on each side, one side having a broad white band and the other side a narrow one. The broad white band should be to the top of the flag on the side nearest the pole.

How to make a secret code

In sending dispatches from one party of Scouts to another it is well to provide against the message falling into the hands of the enemy. Here is a splendid method by which they can be sent without the fear of being read correctly if intercepted by a third party. A piece of cardboard is taken, squares are drawn upon it, and a certain number of the squares are cut out. Each of the sides communicating with one another is provided with a similar piece of cardboard. Now the Scout sending the message places his cardboard on a piece of paper and writes his message in between the spaces cut out and, taking off the cardboard, fills up the paper with any writing he can think of; something that will obscure the real meaning of the message. For instance, the message on the paper may be – "Enemy no longer in supposed ambush. Move stores in morning to thicket one mile and a half to rear. Join you yonder with medical comforts." But with the aid of the cardboard mask the Scouts in the secret will read it as it appears in the illustration.

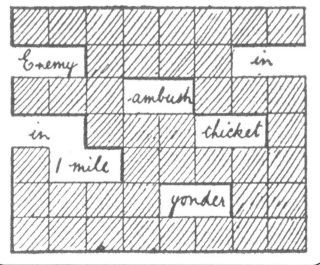

Another useful code

Here is another method none the less ingenious. Below is given the key which one should not find difficult to commit to memory. It will be seen that in each section of the cross three letters of the alphabet are given in their order, except in the last section where only two (Y Z) figure.

A B C	D E F	G H I
J K L	M N O	P Q R
S T U	V W X	Y Z

Now, when you wish to write in the code, you give a section of the cross in which the letter you are using appears and a dot to represent the place of the letter in the section. For instance, supposing you wished to write "Scout" the way you would do so is as follows:

CODE—

SOLUTION— S   C   O   U   T

It must be acknowledged that the code is extremely simple, yet to one not acquainted with the secret it would appear mysterious. Of course Scouts can alter it by changing the positions of the letters.

Ink for dispatches

A Scout has discovered another method of ensuring secrecy in the event of a dispatch bearer being captured by the enemy. The message will be invisible to all not acquainted with the secret of the writing fluid if the following instructions are carried out: dip a pen in an onion and press till the juice comes, then, with plenty of juice on the pen, write your message. If the dispatch gets into the hands of the enemy it will appear to be a blank sheet, but directly it is with your friends, they, being in on the secret, proceed to warm it over the fire, when the writing will stand out clearly.

"The Plimsoll Mark"

You may often have noticed on ships a circular mark with a line running through it. This mark is known as the "Plimsoll Mark". Samuel Plimsoll, "the sailors' friend", devoted the best part of his life to furthering the interests of seafaring men. He noticed that overloaded and unseaworthy vessels were being sent on voyages with very great danger to human life. Consequently he tried to induce Parliament to alter matters; but failing to do so, he himself entered the House of Commons in 1868, and succeeded in getting passed the Merchant Shipping Act in 1876. By this Act the Board of Trade was empowered to detain any vessel deemed unsafe. Finally, owners were ordered to mark upon the sides of their ships a circular disc twelve inches in diameter with a horizontal line eighteen inches long running through it. This line and the centre of the disc mark the line down to which the vessel may be loaded, in salt water.

How to signal by Morse Code

The whole essence of Morse Code is timing. Any method by which a unit of time can be shown, such as shining a torch, waving a flag or blowing a whistle, is suitable to use.

A dot is equal to one beat of time.

A dash is equal to three beats of time.

An interval equal to one dash or three beats is always observed between each letter, or six beats if the end of the word or group.

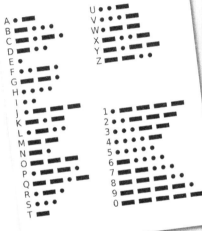

International Morse Code

Therefore the letter a is made by light shown or a flag waved for one beat of time followed by a light shown or flag waved for three beats of time. Then wait before the next letter is started.

Once a letter is started, see it through; don't stop in the middle as it may be misunderstood.

A good signaller, whether fast or slow, will keep a uniform time throughout.

How to communicate by semaphore

When signalling, remember that speed is not everything. If your messages cannot be read, it means double work for everybody. Answer smartly and if asked to reply, do so at once. A good signaller is not made in an hour – stick at it.

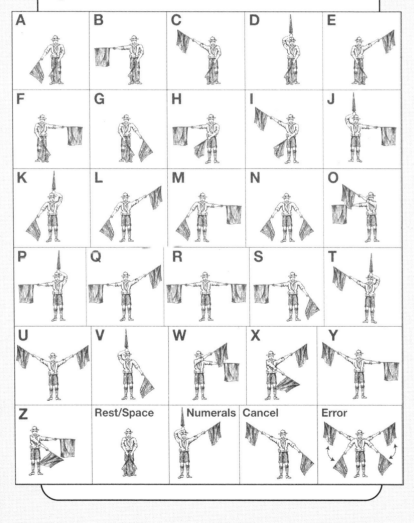

Know your fruits

WILD·FRUITS··

During the summer the flowers in field and hedge have forced themselves upon our notice by their variety of form and colour. The passing of the flower and the falling of the leaves from the trees signify the arrival of autumn – the season of fruits.

The aim of the flower is the production of a seed or seeds which, when properly scattered, will produce new plants when the growing season begins. The seeds are contained in a seed coat, which latter takes many different forms. The seed coat, with the contained seeds, is generally spoken of as the fruit. While the seed is developing, the fruit is generally green and inconspicuous, and often contains an acid substance to protect itself from being carried away by birds and animals. When the seed is matured, the acid substances become sweet and the colour of the fruit changes from green to black, red or brown.

All plants seem to recognise the importance of dispersing their seeds as widely as possible to prevent the overcrowding which might lead to extinction. Wild fruits are divided broadly into two classes – those which split or open to liberate their seeds, and those which do not. The former are termed "dehiscent", and the latter "indehiscent". Among the dehiscent fruits there are really two distinct varieties, the pod-shaped fruit and the box-like fruit. The pod is usually longer than it is broad, although this is not always the case.

The box-like fruits are called capsules, and they are

Plantain Thorn Apple Poppy Campion Dog Violet

exceedingly interesting on account of the various ways in which they open to liberate the ripe seeds. In the Plantain the top of

Hazel

the capsule splits off and falls just as if it were a lid; the Thorn-apple opens by four slits, which extend from the top downwards; while the Poppy, Primrose, etc., have little openings or pores through which the seeds fall as the plant is swayed by the wind.

Hip of Wild Rose

Among the non-splitting fruits we must notice the nut (or achene), which consists of a single seed surrounded

Strawberry

by a very hard coat. This kind of fruit, protruding from a little leafy cup, is familiar to all as the Hazel Nut. The Wild Strawberry is really a collection of little nuts which lie on the surface of a succulent mass. In the case of the Hip the nuts are embedded in the fruit.

Typical Berry

The fruits of the Wake-robin and Barberry are known as berries, the characteristic feature of which is that there are one or more seeds embedded in a pulpy fruit. When there is one large hard seed, or "stone", we call it a stone-fruit or drupe, e.g. Wild Plum.

Typical Stone fruit

Finally, we have the winged fruits, called samaras, and the tufted fruits. The wing is usually brown and leaf-like in appearance, and varies in size and shape according to the weight of seed it is designed to carry. The hairy or tufted seeds are generally much smaller than those with wings.

Cuckoo Pint

In order to know wild fruits we must go out at the right season and study them first-hand. It is an excellent idea to make a collection.

Beware of the breakwaters

Breakwaters are often erected around cliffs which, being of soft sandstone, are, through the washing of the sea, likely to fall. These breakwaters, which run far into the sea, are, of course, hidden from view, and would be a source of danger to ships passing by. To prevent accidents, however, posts, as depicted in our illustration, are erected at intervals, warning ships to keep well outside of them.

Tells when there's fire

Many ships have a pipe running from the hold to the deck, as shown in the illustration. It is a precaution against fire. If even a trifling fire occurs in the hold smoke will ascend the pipe, and upon issuing from the top will be noticed by some of the crew. Checking it would then be comparatively easy. In the absence of a pipe a fire might begin and remain unnoticed until it assumed such proportions that conquering it would be almost impossible.

Be Fit

Baden-Powell says in *Scouting for Boys*, "Alertness of the body means alertness of the mind." It's certainly true that plenty of exercise and fresh air provide oxygen to the brain and inspire clear thinking. But there's no need to stick to dull exercises – why not get involved in a team game such as cricket, or learn to swim?

It's equally important to eat healthily and pay attention to personal hygiene. Sometimes it's the tiniest bugs that wreak the worst havoc. "Take care of your body," said Jim Rohn, "it's the only place you have to live."

How to catch a ball

A good fieldsman must always be ready for the ball to come his way. Practise the methods described below and you won't be called "Butterfingers".

Catch the ball close to the body. Have your hands turned upwards. Never be nervous, and if you are uncertain, field close in at practice for a few days, and confidence will return.

An expert says that for catching the hands should be slightly overlapping. This is to prevent the shock of the impact forcing the hands apart. The fingers should be slightly bent upwards. This is to form a natural cup for the ball to fall into, and makes the closing of the hands a quicker movement.

The hands should be held about four inches away from the chest. As the ball enters the hands and these close on it, they should be allowed to sink on the body, in which position the catch is finally held. This is to allow a gradual lessening of the force of the impact, which minimises the chance of the ball jumping after contact.

Fielding Tip

Excellent advice has been given to young players. The expert says: "Always back-up the man who will receive the ball close to the wicket. Always try for a catch however difficult it may seem. Always be on the look-out and ready for the ball. Run at top speed towards the ball directly it is hit. Use both hands. Obey your captain cheerfully and promptly. Never hesitate about taking up the position assigned to you."

How to play some cricket shots

The Cut

The real genuine cut goes to the left side of point – if point stands in a line with the wicket. The ball is hit when it has reached a spot nearly in a line with the wicket and the length of the ball is rather short. If far up it is a ball to drive and not to cut. You must have a strong wrist and the power of timing.

There is the forward cut where the ball pitches outside the off-stump. Do not move the right foot, but bring the left foot across the wicket. This is a beautiful stroke, but one of the most difficult to bring off. The late cut is when the ball has passed you, and you put all your wrist power into the stroke. The square cut comes from a ball travelling square with the batsman. Remember that no ball that could possibly hit the wicket should be cut!

The Drive

Then there is the drive. There are three distinct varieties of the off-drive – between point and cover; between cover and mid-off; and the drive to long-off, with a well-pitched-up ball, not necessarily a half-volley. The timing can be driven with more force than almost any stroke. Left-handers as a rule utilise this stroke more frequently than right-handers.

To keep the ball on the ground is a golden rule; but it does not follow that the ball should never be lifted. Runs from brilliant drives on the off-side are saved time after time by smart fieldsmen through the ball being kept down. If you occasionally lift a ball over mid-off or extra cover's head the risk run is not very great.

How to make a punching-bag

There are fewer better exercises than that which the punching-ball affords, and such an appliance is really quite cheap and easy to make. The muscles of the arms and chest are splendidly

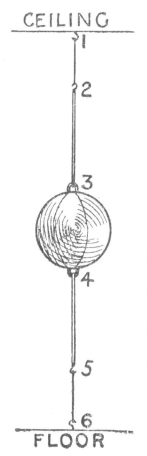

developed by the punching-ball, and the apparatus can easily be erected in almost any home as it takes up little enough space.

It is necessary to have two pieces of moulded rubber cord, ¼ or ⅜ of an inch in diameter, and about 12 in. long. Then get two pieces of very strong wire ⅛ of an inch in diameter, and 4 in. long, and bend each end carefully over. Now fasten one end of each of the two pieces of rubber cord to the pieces of wire. This is done by inserting the end of the rubber into the bend of the wire, and then closing the bend as much as possible by using a pair of pincers. You will find the wire grips the rubber very firmly. The next process is making the bag. This should be made of canvas. Cut the canvas into four oblong pieces, sew together all but one seam, then stuff the ball. If the ball is to be used by a beginner, it is advisable to stuff it with hay or straw; if not a beginner, paper torn small and well pressed together is better. Now finish seaming the ball, and at each end (

make a loop of either leather or several pieces of canvas made into a strip, and sew on to the ball. Make a special note of sewing these loops on very firmly, for you must remember that this is the point where the strain will most particularly be felt. One piece of rubber is hooked on to each loop, and the ball is suspended between the ceiling and floor of the room, copper wire or thick string being used to give the ball a suitable height. Our diagram shows the ball ready for punching; 2, 3, and 4, 5, are the pieces of rubber cord, 1, 2, and 5, 6, are the pieces of wire or cord to regulate the height; 1 and 6 are hooks screwed into the ceiling and floor respectively. Of course, such a home-made punching-ball as that described does not equal the expensive article, but, considering how cheaply it can be constructed, it is most useful and effective.

How to get a strong grip

If you wish to develop the muscles of your hand to give you an "iron grip", you can do so without purchasing any elaborate equipment.

Ask the nearest garage people to give you a piece of old motor tyre about five inches long. You will find that the rubber fabric, if not too thin, possesses great resiliency, and at first it will tire your hand to bend it even a few times.

How to do breast-stroke

It is better, if possible, to get a parent who is a swimmer to go into the water with you. He will hold your chin up, and tell you when you are going wrong. It used to be said that the sea is the best place to learn to swim. Salt water weighs a great deal more than fresh water, and is therefore better able to keep you afloat. But as it is not possible for every Scout to take his lessons in the sea, I will assume that you attend the local swimming baths.

The first thing to attempt is the arm movements. Wade out until the water is nearly up to your armpits. Now extend your arms until your hands are straight in front of you and under the water. Keep your hands close together.

Are you ready? Good! Keeping your arms as stiff as you possibly can, take them outwards and round in a semi-circle towards the body.

Now, as your elbows brush your sides, bring your hands under your chin, keeping them pointing forward. You have completed the stroke. Repeat this as many times as you like until you get used to the movement.

As soon as you find that by doing this you move forward in the water, you can commence to use your feet and combine the leg with the arm movements.

Bending both knees and pushing them outwards, you also extend your arms. Now kick open your legs as wide as possible and bring them together again. The hands should be outwards when the ankles touch.

The legs are now drawn up, and the leg

movements gone through again as soon as you bring your hands under your chin.

If you follow these tips carefully and perfect the strokes, you should have very little difficulty in learning to swim.

The picture shows quite clearly how you should appear in the water when doing the breast-stroke. You will notice that the boy's body is entirely under water. Only his head is showing above. Keep your hands and arms well under the water; take your strokes carefully – don't be in a hurry; and remain as low as possible in the water.

How to swim under water

To swim under water one should practise in a methodical way. Most beginners take a deep breath and then swim about in a careless fashion until they feel themselves short of breath.

This is the correct way to gain confidence and to increase the length of time during which you can stay under water. Take several deep breaths and then expel every particle of air from the lungs, immediately following up with a full deep breath. Now make a deeper dive than you usually make. When under water take regular strokes of, say, one a second, and count them; try to go one stroke farther each time.

This idea of counting and gradually increasing the number of strokes will give you great confidence, and will also enable you to judge roughly how far from land you will come to the surface.

Swimming exercises

The water should be your friend rather than your enemy if you are to become a good swimmer.

An excellent method of gaining confidence is to throw a coin into clear water about four feet deep and then try to pick it up. As you attempt this you will find that that water seems to be pushing against you, which proves its buoyancy.

An excellent method of gaining confidence is to throw a coin into clear water about four feet deep and then try to pick it up

To accomplish this feat you will have to keep your eyes open under water. They may smart a little at first, but the water will do them no harm, and the fact of being able to see under the water will put you at your ease and make you feel still more confident.

Another exercise is done in this way. Take your stand in water up to your shoulders. Draw in a deep breath and then bend the knees until your head is completely under water. See how long you can stay under before you need a second breath. Increase the time at each attempt. When you have succeeded in staying under for a fairly long period you can attempt a dive with confidence.

Bedtime exercises for you!

While unbuttoning and removing your coat, bend backwards and forwards as far as possible. This exercises the muscles of the abdomen.

While removing your waistcoat bend far to one side and then to the other to strengthen the muscles of the sides.

As you untie your tie and take off your collar, raise your body and lower it by bending the knees. This will keep the muscles of the upper legs supple.

For exercising the calves raise and lower the body by standing first on your toes and then on your heels. Do this while taking your braces off.

For exercising the calves raise and lower the body by standing first on your toes and then on your heels. Do this while taking your braces off

Next comes the shirt. Raise and lower your shoulders while slipping it off. This will help to keep muscles of the central top part of your shoulders in the right fettle.

Raise left and right legs while slipping off trousers, if possible. This strengthens the upper part of your abdomen.

While performing the above exercises breathe deeply and slowly.

Health hints

Clean bodies mean sound bodies! A body must be clean within and without.

✔ Let the stomach rest between meals.

✔ Exercise your limbs before going to bed.

✔ Clean wounds, scratches and bruises heal rapidly. They should be thoroughly cleansed with hot water and bound with clean (boiled) rag or sterilised bandage.

✔ The sun is a splendid tonic.

✔ A little soda water will relieve sick head-ache caused by indigestion.

Health Rhyme (1)

Poison clings in dirty nails,
So keep them short and clean,
Daily scrub, trim now and then,
And this good health will mean.

Health Rhyme (2)

Neck, ears and nails all need a rub,
Each morning when you rise,
The same again before you sleep
And health will be your prize.

How to jump

Do you know the correct way to jump? You may seriously hurt yourself by jumping in the wrong manner from a height and it is possible to fracture your skull from the shock of the jump.

An accident like this would be termed indirect violence and it is due to the shock of the fall being directed through the heels up through the legs and thighs, and so on through the pelvis, to the skull, which, if the shock is strong enough will crack.

Look at the sketch and you will see the correct way to jump. Jump straight off with the heels well raised and then as you land bend the knees forward to counteract the shock.

Be Yourself

Sometimes being prepared is more of a state of mind than anything else. Have you ever noticed how much better you are performing tasks when you are feeling happy and confident? There's no great secret to gaining this confidence, other than approaching life with a positive attitude. Get on with things instead of complaining about them. Tackle the most difficult tasks first, and as every Scout knows, "always do your best". Above all, don't try and fit in with the crowd In order to be something you're not – if you believe in something different, follow your instincts, do your own thing and be yourself.

How to be brave

If ever you feel afraid of doing something that it is right to do, make yourself do it; and then do it again and again until you find yourself doing it without any hesitation.

You may not like diving into cold water or going through the woods on a dark night, but you should force yourself to do it a few times until you find that you don't mind it.

When you are in a funk you must not on any account show it. Then is the time to whistle and smile as if you liked it. The bravest of all are those who, while feeling worried, are so strong-minded that they conquer their fear and don't allow it to show itself to others.

You may not like diving into cold water or going through the woods on a dark night, but you should force yourself to do it a few times until you find that you don't mind it.

How to overcome difficulties

When you see an impossible-looking job before you, go at it, "grin and tackle it" and ten to one you will come out triumphant in the end, and all the more happy because it was difficult.

The whole excitement of life is facing difficulties and dangers and apparent impossibilities, and in the end getting a chance of attaining the summit of the mountain.

Life would pall if it were all sugar; salt is bitter if taken by itself, but when tasted as part of the dish, it savours the meat. Difficulties are the salt of life.

If things at any time look difficult for you, or even impossible, think of a way by which you might have won success and then figure to yourself your winning it.

Whenever a difficulty comes your way, even if it be the biggest difficulty in the world, tackle it cheerily and pluckily, and if you can't get over it one way, try another and stick to it till you are successful.

When you are up against the blank wall of difficulty, remember: though it looks high at first sight, closer investigation may show cracks and crannies by which you may surmount it; and, even if it cannot be scaled, ten to one there is a way round.

When in danger or worry or illness or even a bit of hard work, you will find that, if you force yourself to smile, half the difficulty will disappear.

A Scout whistles when in difficulties

When there is danger before you, don't stop and look at it – the more you look at it the less you will like it – but take the plunge, go boldly in at it, and it won't be half as bad as it looked, when you are once in it.

St. George was typical of what a Scout should be. When he was faced by a great difficulty or danger, however great it appeared, he did not avoid it or fear it, but went at it with all the power he could put into himself and his horse.

Some men are born brave, others require to have courage thrust upon them. But in the large majority of cases it is a quality which can be cultivated.

How to do your best

No man can do more than his best.

Try to leave this world a little better than you found it and, when your turn comes to die, you can die happy in feeling that at any rate you have not wasted your time but have done your best.

Make hay whenever your sun shines. Don't wait for it to shine later on, clouds may get worse and rainy times set in.

How to be good

By "doing good" I mean making yourself useful and doing small kindnesses to other people – whether they be friends or strangers. It is not a difficult matter, and the best way to set about it is to make up your mind to do at least one "good turn" to somebody every day, and you will soon get into the habit of doing good turns always. It does not matter how small the "good turn" may be – even if it is only to help an old person across the street, or say a good word for somebody who is being badly spoken of. The great thing is to do something.

Something good ought to be done each day of your life.

Do your Good Turn not only to your friends, but to strangers, and even to your enemies.

When you have done a good thing, don't hang about to be thanked or to be made a hero of, get away quietly and unnoticed.

If you stick to it and force yourself to do something good day by day, it very soon grows into a habit with you and you then find how many little things you can do which all count as good turns although small in themselves.

The smile and the Good Turn are our speciality. The want of

> **It does not matter how small the "good turn" may be – even if it is only to help an old person across the street, or say a good word for somebody who is being badly spoken of.**

these in the average citizen is at the root of much of our social trouble today.

The beauty about good turns: they may seem small when you do them, but you can never see where they are going to end.

How to be happy

The only true success is happiness.

There are two keys to happiness:

Do not take things too seriously, but make the best of what you have got, and look on life as a game and the world as a playground.

Let your actions and thoughts be directed by love.

Happiness is within the reach of everyone, rich or poor. Yet comparatively few people are happy.

Many people think that "pleasure" is the same thing as "happiness". That's where they take the wrong turning.

A joyful home, coupled with the ability to serve others, gives the best happiness. I believe that we were sent into this world to enjoy life and I defy any idler to do that.

The royal road to happiness is through brotherhood and service, plus appreciation of nature, coupled with a sense of humour.

Happiness does not come by sitting down and waiting for it.

It is only through goodwill and co-operation – that is, through service for others – that someone reaches true success, which is happiness. For then they find that heaven is here in this world, and not merely a vision of the next.

They are happiest who can look back with fewest regrets.

Remember, no matter how badly off you are in wealth or health, you can always bring a ray of cheer into other people's lives, and in so doing you bring the best kind of happiness into your own.

The real way to get happiness is by giving out happiness to other people.

Make the best of what you've got and don't go crying for the moon.

No matter how badly off you are in wealth or health, you can always bring a ray of cheer into other people's lives, and in so doing you bring the best kind of happiness into your own.

How to lead

Leadership is the keynote to success – but leadership is difficult to define, and leaders are difficult to find. I have frequently stated that "anyone can be a commander, and a trained man may often make an instructor; but a leader is more like the poet – born, not manufactured."

There are four essential points to look for in a leader:

• A leader must have wholehearted faith and belief in the rightness of the cause.

• A leader must have a cheery, energetic personality, with sympathy and friendly understanding of his or her followers.

• A leader must have confidence in themselves through knowing the job.

• What a leader preaches he or she must practise.

The essentials of leadership might, in telegraphic brevity, be summed up as "comradeship and competence".

The difference between a leader and a commander: almost any fool can command, can make people obey orders, if he has adequate power of punishment at his back to support him in case of refusal. It is another thing to lead, to carry men with you in a big job.

"Come on", rather than "Go on", when you want a job done.

How to persevere

When things look bad, just smile and sing to yourself, as the thrush sings: "Stick to it, stick to it, stick to it", and you will come through all right.

A very great step to success is to be able to stand disappointments.

A real Scout is always patient: they don't worry if they don't succeed all at once, but wait and work quietly and determinedly till they "get there" in the end – in small things just as much as in big ones.

"The oak was once an acorn." If ever you feel hopeless about getting on to success in life from a small beginning, remember that even that great strong tree, the oak, began at first as a little acorn lying on the ground.

Never say die till you are dead. Struggle on against any difficulty or danger, don't give in to it, and you will probably come out successful in the end.

When your mind tells you that it is impossible, reply to it: "No, not impossible; I see what might be – I can try; I can win it, I can, I can, I can, and I will!" And ten to one you will succeed.

Nothing is impossible, except putting the toothpaste back into the tube.

How to be sportsmanlike

A sportsman always keeps his temper under the most exciting and provoking circumstances. In all games you must learn not to be upset or bad-tempered if you lose. Try your best throughout the game, but never say or even allow yourself to think: "The other side won, but we were the better team!" A good sportsman takes losses without grumbling or worrying and, when beaten, is always ready to give the victor the credit due.

Never criticise the referee's decisions. Every referee makes mistakes; in fact, every human being does. If you cannot play your games in a real sporting spirit, you are best to leave them alone.

Never criticise the referee's decisions. Every referee makes mistakes; in fact, every human being does. So if you feel a grudge against a referee, try to referee one or two games yourself, and you will soon sympathise with him in his task.

During the games, the strictest rules are observed, which mean self-restraint and good temper on the part of the players, and at the end it is the proper form that the victor should sympathise with the one who is conquered, and that the opponent should be the first to cheer and congratulate the winner. This should be made the practice until it becomes the habit.

If you cannot play your games in a real sporting spirit, you are best to leave them alone altogether.

Are you ready?

Are you ready to run to the assistance of a person injured in an accident? Would you know how to deal with a mad dog if you

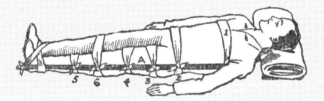

chanced to meet one? Could you take over the work of nursing a sick person at a moment's notice? You ought to know how to do so, if you're a Scout.

Remember our motto, "Be Prepared"; you never know what may happen.

Robert Baden-Powell

Chief Scout

Don't
Try This at Home

Times change, and advice that once seemed
sensible and helpful can now look positively
hare-brained. Here you will find a selection of
hints and tips that have dated rather less well
down the years, from how to split water to how
to make a safety lamp that is anything but safe.
No Scouts were harmed in the making of this
book, and we wouldn't want to start now.
Therefore we should state for the record: none
of this should be attempted in the home or
anywhere else. As a wise old owl once said,
"Accidents hurt; safety doesn't." You
have been warned!

How to stop your fixed-wheel bike without a brake

Even in these days of cheap free-wheel bicycles there are many cyclists who, from force of circumstances or for other reasons, ride bicycles with fixed wheels. Here is a hint for them if at any time they are riding downhill on a brakeless machine, or if their brake is out of order. In going down an incline, the bicycle, of course, tries its utmost to run away, and in pressing on the rising pedals to check this, the rider is lifted off his saddle at each revolution, and this fails to slacken his speed. To prevent this, pass the right hand round and grip the back of the saddle; the body is thus held down, enabling back-pedalling to be continued. Try this next time you find yourself brake-less; you will be surprised at the effectiveness of the method.

How to split water

Chemists often call in electricity to their aid and it is fairly simple to do an experiment involving "electrolysis" as it is called. You require a good robust 6-volt battery or better still, if you can borrow one, a 6-volt accumulator! Three-quarters fill a tumbler with water and add a good teaspoonful of washing soda. Now take an old torch battery to pieces and extract two carbon rods, the black things which go down the centre. Scrape the tops clean and attach by wires, one to the positive terminal of your battery, the other to the negative terminal. Now place in the tumbler of solution, but don't let them touch under the surface. Bubbles will come from each rod. One rod will give off oxygen, the other will give off hydrogen. In other words, you have split up the water. You can work the same experiment with water made slightly acid by putting in a little of the liquid from inside the accumulator. Perhaps a garage will sell you a little. For batteries it is rather dilute but even so it will burn a hole in your clothes if you leave it on for some time.

How to waterproof a tent

Cut up two pounds of paraffin wax into two gallons of turpentine. Place the vessel containing this into a pail of hot water until the wax is melted, stirring occasionally. Set the tent up, and paint with the hot solution, working it rapidly, and using a stiff brush. Do this on a sunny morning and leave the tent standing until dry. Turpentine is flammable, so keep it away from the flames!

A Scouting ruse

Most Scouts know of the method which the Native American of North America adopts when he wishes to hear sounds of man or beast that may be some distance away.

He lies flat upon the ground and applies his ear to the earth, and by this means he is able to distinguish clearly sounds which otherwise would be quite inaudible. We can hardly possess the keen hearing of the Native American, but we can learn from their methods. This improvement is effected by opening the two blades of a penknife, and, sticking the larger blade into the ground, placing the ear against the short one. Movements on the ground set up vibrations in the metal, which are in turn conducted to the ear. Scouts when practising this should be very careful. Stick the knife in the ground after lying down, as one might easily jerk one's ear against the open blade and perhaps cause a serious injury.

We can hardly possess the keen hearing of the Native American, but we can learn from their methods

SECTION.

Cowboy horsemanship

Among the finest, if not the finest, horsemen of the world are the cowboys of the West of the United States, and their steeds are so trained that horse and rider may well be said to be as one. The horses are invaluable for hunting, rounding up cattle, and are still more valuable in the daily perils and emergencies the cowboy is called upon to face. Our picture shows a horse trained to enable the cowboy, who is invariably a dead shot, to fire behind at a pursuing enemy. When going at full speed the horse, on command, will rein up suddenly and lie upon the ground. The cowboy then unslings his rifle, turns round in the saddle until he can use the horse's back as a rest, and takes careful aim. He then jumps up, allows his horse to rise, and again

gallops off at full speed. Horses who are "old stagers" at this game usually find opportunity to snatch a few mouthfuls of grass during the interval which occurs in alighting and firing.

How to climb a pole

When you are out Scouting you may find it necessary to obtain a clear view of the surrounding country, and a Scout who can climb a tree or post quickly is of great use to his party.

Many trees have low branches which enable the climber to get a firm grip, but others which are quite bare at the base are much more difficult to climb.

A good way in which to overcome this difficulty is to tie your ankles together with your neckerchief. You will find that it gives you greater strength for swarming up the tree or post.

The neckerchief should be tied as illustrated, but not too tightly.

How to cure a rabbit skin

To cure a rabbit skin, let the skin steep in cold water for twenty-four hours, then take it out, clean it well and remove all the fat. Now prepare the mixture for curing the skin: three pounds of powdered alum and four ounces of rock salt dissolved in as much water as will cover the skin. Boil it and allow it to cool; when lukewarm, place the skin in it and leave it for four days, working it well with the hands every day (wear protective gloves). After that time has elapsed, take out the skin and dry it in an airy place, but not in the sun. Boil up the liquid again and repeat the process. Afterwards, wash the skin well in clean water, changing the water several times. Then beat the skin with a wooden mallet until it is soft.

How to engrave your knife

A Scout's knife is one of his most treasured possessions and a proved companion in many a tight corner. Every Scout should guard against losing such a treasure by engraving his name upon it. The method is extremely simple. First coat the blade all over with beeswax, and with some sharp pointed instrument –

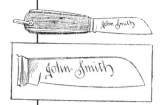

preferably a needle or pen-nib – write your name upon it, then apply some strong nitric acid to the writing, taking care not to let it touch any steel part not covered with the beeswax. Next sprinkle some table salt upon the acid and allow it to remain for ten minutes. Then wash off the beeswax and salt and the name will appear clearly engraved upon the blade. When handling the acid take great care not to let it drop upon your clothes, as it would quickly burn them.

How to seal cracked soles

Wearers of tennis shoes are often troubled by the appearance of a large crack across the rubber sole of the shoe. This may be repaired in the following manner:

Obtain a metal skewer and heat it. Do not let it get too hot, though. Now push the hot iron into the crack, moving it backwards and forwards as you do so. After a time the rubber will melt and when the affected part is quite soft remove the skewer and pinch the sides of the crack together, holding the shoe tightly until the rubber becomes cool and sets hard.

Re-heat the skewer and pass it over the top of the crack until all signs of a hole have disappeared.

How to write on glass

Very little apparatus is required to enable one to write one's name or engrave some device upon a piece of glass. The main requirements are a leaden saucer (easily constructed out of a piece of sheet-lead), some fluorspar (fluoride of calcium) and strong sulphuric acid, both of which can be obtained from the chemist.

Powder some of your fluorspar in the saucer and add some of the sulphuric acid to it. Next take your glass and coat it with wax. On the wax inscribe your name or device with a needle point or some sharp instrument. Then place the glass, waxed side downwards, upon the saucer. For a minute or two apply a gentle heat to the saucer, taking care not to melt the wax.

When the wax is wiped off, your device should appear engraved upon the glass.

The acid formed by the two chemicals is called hydrofluoric acid, and possesses the property of attacking glass. When working with it be careful not to let any of it drop on to your clothes, as it possesses the property of attacking them also in a very unpleasant manner.

How to write in fire

Here is a method by which letters of fire can be traced upon paper. Supposing the selected writing to be "The Scout". Well, you commence by procuring a strong solution of saltpetre, and in this dip the "wrong end" of a penholder. Then with it write the words, taking care that the penholder is all the time supplied with the fluid, and that the continuity of the writing is nowhere broken. Double up the two ends of the paper to raise it from the ground, as shown in the illustration, and apply a glowing match to some spot touched by the writing. A tiny glow-worm of red light will then travel along the paper, following the lines of your writing, until "The Scout" is traced.

How to make paper transparent

All who have occasion to make use of tracing paper may manufacture it for themselves by damping the paper to be employed with pure, fresh-distilled benzine. So long as the benzine remains in its substance, the paper is transparent, and will permit of tracing being made in writing or water colour on its surface without any running. However, as the benzine evaporates, the paper recovers its opacity, and if the drawing is not completed before this happens it will be necessary to damp the paper again. The fact that the paper again becomes opaque is an advantage over the ordinary tracing paper, which is flimsy and unmanageable. Even stout drawing paper can be made transparent by the above process. A word of caution. When handling the benzine be careful that no artificial light is near and do not make use of the benzine or keep the bottle in a room with a high temperature.

How to make a phosphorus safety lamp

The first necessity for a night watchman is generally supposed to be a good lantern of some kind, but when he happens to be employed in a powder magazine this rather alters the case. You can make a light which combines absolute safety with sufficient illumination to read the time by a watch and other things in the following manner. Place a piece of phosphorus about the size of a pea in a small bottle of clear glass. Then fill the latter one-third full of the  best olive oil heated to boiling point, and cork it tightly. When a light is required the cork should be removed to allow the air to enter, and then replaced. The whole of the empty space will at once become luminous.

How to stop a runaway horse carriage

The way to stop a runaway horse is not to run out in front of it and wave your arms, as so many people do, but to try and race alongside it, catch hold of the shaft to keep yourself from falling, and seize the reins with the other hand.

Why you should keep pigs

Everybody should keep one or more pigs, because as you will see from the accompanying sketch, everything except a pig's grunt can be utilised.

Always keep your pigsty clean; a pig cannot thrive in a dirty sty. Give your pig good, clean, dry bedding, such as wheat-straw, grass or bracken. Collect house refuse such as potato peelings, outside cabbage leaves, etc., and ask your neighbours to keep a swill-tub for you.

A field filter

Scouts in Great Britain, when they become thirsty on the move, have never far to go out of their way to find water which is fairly pure and when boiled will be fit for anyone to drink. Still a Scout should know how to look after himself anywhere and be equal to any emergency. Supposing a Troop or Patrol were so placed that their only water supply consisted of the liquid contained by the average ditch. They would have of necessity to drink it to satisfy their thirst, but if they possessed a bucket of some description, a little sand, and a few stones, there should be no reason for them not drinking their water in a fairly pure condition by constructing the filter shown in the diagram. It is made as follows: a hole is drilled in the bottom of the bucket, and into it is inserted a piece of tubing of fairly large bore. Then place in the vessel A, large stones; B, small stones; C, coarse sand; D, fine sand. Fill the rest of the receptacle with the muddy water, and after a time it will filter through in a clear state ready for boiling and drinking.

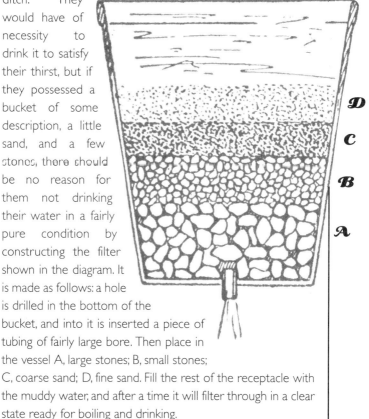

Section of Filter

D

C

B

A

Join the Adventure

Scouting offers fun, friendship and everyday adventure to 400,000 boys and girls aged 6–25 in the UK. Scouting has a positive impact on young people, its 100,000 volunteers as well as local and national communities. From abseiling and archery, to music, craft and drama and leadership experience, Scouting offers life-changing opportunities that help young people become the active citizens of the future.

Our young people...

- Get to make friends and try new things
- Earn badges and awards, including the Duke of Edinburgh's Awards
- Try over 200 different adventurous activities
- Get to camp, travel overseas and meet Scouts across the world
- Learn Scouting skills and pass them on
- Lead small teams, learn team-building skills and do other things that look great on a CV

Our volunteers...

- Give over 364 million hours to volunteer within their communities
- Are contributing to an international movement that has 31 million members in 218 countries around the world
- Benefit from training and personal development

Our challenge...

- Even with 100,000 adult volunteers we still have over 30,000 young people on waiting lists across the country waiting to take part in Scouting
- And that is where you come in. We are looking for

enthusiastic adult volunteers who can help us offer adventure and opportunities for more young people within their local communities… and to join the adventure themselves!

- Whether you have several hours a week or a year or you are looking for a one-off volunteering project, there are opportunities for you to contribute. With roles ranging from leader to treasurer, website designer to volunteer manager, we offer opportunities based on the time you can give and your skills and interests

Did you know?

- There are now half a million members of Scouting in the UK
- Scouting in the UK has been growing for the last seven years
- More young people do adventurous activities as Scouts than with any other organisation
- Each year Scouts spend over two million nights away from home doing adventurous activities
- The youngest person to walk to the South Pole was a Scout
- Each year Scouts tackling the Queen's Scout Award walk the equivalent distance of once around the world
- 11 of the 12 people to walk on the moon were once Scouts
- John Lennon and Paul McCartney were both Scouts (inspiring a better quality of campfire song)
- You are rarely more than 10 miles from a Scout Meeting Place

www.scouts.org.uk

The Scout Association, Registered Charity no. 306101 (England and Wales) and SC038437 (Scotland).

Acknowledgements

Thank you to Stuart Cooper, Claire Potter and Jolyon Braime as well as Claire Woodforde, Daniel Scott-Davies, Nicola Gordon-Wilson and Chris James at The Scout Association.

The Essential Camping Cookbook or How to Cook an Egg in an Orange and other Scout Recipes

The essential guide to cooking outdoors, whether you're camping, 'glamping', at a festival or on the beach.

Drawing on the know-how and expertise of The Scout Association, this inspirational cookbook takes the art of eating outdoors to a whole new level and is perfect for beginners to al fresco cooking as well as seasoned campers.

Alongside traditional campfire favourites, you will find more than 80 recipes for curries, spicy stews, exotic barbecues and one-pot dishes. There are also recipes from well-known celebrities including Stephen Fry and Michael Palin.

There is comprehensive information to explain all the essential techniques needed to make a glorious feast – including how to cook backwoods-style, without conventional equipment, on open fires, in pit ovens and using improvised utensils.

Now turn to the popular campfire songs at the back and your outdoor eating experience will be complete!

ISBN 978-1-47110-054-3